A Gift of Healing

in a Handbook

A Gift of Healing

IN A HANDBOOK

PENNEY LEYSHON
KATHLEEN SPELLMAN

OXCCIDUS SM LLC

OXCCIDUS SM LLC

Title: A Gift of Healing in a Handbook
Authors: Penney Leyshon and Kathleen Spellman
Copyright © 2005 Oxccidus SM LLC All rights reserved.
First Edition

ISBN: 0-9760286-0-3
Library of Congress Control Number: 2004114238

Published in the United States of America by Oxccidus LLC
P.O. Box 274, Rowayton, CT 06853
www.oxccidus.com   info@oxccidus.com

Printed in the United States of America by Brody Printing Co., Inc.
Bridgeport, CT 06607

Dictionary definitions are used with permission of
Merriam-Webster Online Dictionary © 2004 by Merriam-Webster,
Incorporated (www.Merriam-Webster.com).

Photographs and Original artwork: Penney Leyshon
Poems and Quotations: Penney Leyshon
Cover Design and Layout: Jennifer Ditacchio
Editors: Louise Ladd & Catharine Labine
Pyramid of Being Design: Massimo De'Rossi

This book reflects the opinions of the authors, and does not dispense, nor is it intended to be a substitute for, medical advice or treatment. It is provided with the understanding that the reader should consult a medical or other appropriate professional for any medical advice or treatment.
In the event you use any of the information in this book for yourself, which is your constitutional right, the authors and the publisher assume no responsibility for your actions.
A Gift of Healing in a Handbook

*This Book
is Dedicated to
Everyone*

CONTENTS

A GIFT OF HEALING
IN A HANDBOOK

TABLE OF CONTENTS

PART I
HUMANITY

CHAPTER 1

CHAPTER 2

PART II
THE IDEAS OF HEALING

CHAPTER 3

CHAPTER 4

CONTENTS

PART III
THE GAME & THE ART

THE SPIRITUAL WORLD WITH EARTH

*We often appear to be totally unaware
that the spiritual world can weave in and out
of our Earth, creating a bond. However, this
spiritual world is accessible to us at any time. It
has the force to work through the Earth world to
touch our souls with such strength that nothing is
beyond us.*

FOREWORD

Since my career first began, I have been writing the material for this book. I would jot down information as it surfaced in my mind: after a work session, when a client left me, while taking walks and in the middle of the night.

In September of 1990, my entire life shifted dramatically within 24 hours. I have experienced many initiatory processes into the world of healing, so when this particular devastating episode occurred, I stayed as calm and as open as I could.

As years have passed, through the vehicle of relentless repetitive sound, and a disrupted existence in time, the spaces and levels of reality that have been revealed, and made available to me, have been monumental.

Story after story could be told.

But, with regard to this book, I will tell you: this process and segment of my life has been horrific; and yet, at the same time, sacred. Beyond its pain, this "alteration" has allowed me to delve deeper into knowledge of the self, this world and the universe.

Penney Leyshon

A GIFT OF HEALING

"We are here to heal ourselves and to heal the world."

Although the knowledge offered by Penney Leyshon is universal, it is also original. The information presented in this book comes directly to her through her mind and soul. Her experience and her journey are her own.

INTRODUCTION

A Gift of Healing in a Handbook heals as it teaches. This book is designed for people who do not understand or are afraid of crisis, life and death. It presents hope as a reality and provides answers.

There is a healing that takes place in the body and in the soul. It is one of the main reasons we are here on Earth - to learn, to grow and to discover. Another reason that we're here is to experience life as a being of wholeness, and to learn not to be afraid of what that means.

In this book, professional healer and artist Penney Leyshon demystifies the "ABC's" of spiritual healing by sharing universal wisdom about living, dying, seeking and finding; an understanding that comes directly to her through a remarkable psychic gift.

Part of Penney Leyshon does not live on this plane, yet she is also here. Penney is very much in tune with the universe. Her connection with it is direct, active and far-reaching through space and time. When you hear her words or interact with her on this level, it is clear that she is a traveler and is not in sync with our time. Life has been uncomfortable and often confusing for Penney because she lives in an altered state, (or between both worlds) half *here* and half *there*. Yet, she has a sharp sense of humor and is not a sensationalist.

This book is presented to the world at a crucial time

in our existence. Penney Leyshon gently takes us by the hand and brings us out into the universe. As a teacher, she shows us how to observe our humanity from a more expansive perspective. We are offered insights and explanations for why we are here, why we are meant to go through our experiences, and how we will move forward and advance as beings. Although our deepest fears, struggles and traumas are very real to us, we are comforted by the assurance that there is purpose to everything we face. From a place we are evolving to, we are presented with the *whole* picture and with a vision of the possibilities for ourselves in the future.

Penney has the gift of sight. Her healing gift is one of transformational energy and information. Within seconds, she is able to move, sift through, direct, dissect and make sense of the continuous stream of data as it floods through her like water bursting through a dam. Much like a scientist, she is able to translate and transmute the information to our vibrational level, our time frame. Penney's gift is used clearly, practically and purposefully with full respect for the world to which it is being delivered.

The photographs, photos of paintings and the text in this book carry healing energy. They establish integrity and promote creativity by opening channels to new ways of thinking. In addition, the quotations and poems herein are all Penney Leyshon's original work.

Within each chapter we have used, with permission, standard dictionary definitions from the Merriam-Webster Dictionary, as a quick reference tool.

A Gift of Healing in a Handbook shows us as readers a way to begin a journey of discovery. It helps us to go deeper and learn the truth about who we are. The intent is to shed light on a process within each of us that carries itself beyond this life.

I have often been asked, "So, what exactly was your role in the writing of this book?"

It was twofold. First, Penney and I both transcribed the book from our telephone sessions, all of which were taped.

Second, I have always been a student and lover of foreign languages. I am an interpreter who has also been trained in the art of asking questions. I have endeavored to translate the ideas and knowledge of Penney Leyshon. There were many times when this was a mystifying and challenging task.

When Penney speaks, she is very deliberate about the way she says something. She intentionally presents broad, open-ended meanings with her words. She tries to establish a base for ideas so that they can be absorbed in many ways and on many levels. Sometimes it was very difficult for both of us to find a middle ground between the ideas she was trying to put across and how I thought people would interpret them. My priority was to translate her knowledge in its purest form. Parts of this book put forth information that bends the construction of conventional limited language. No compromises were made in the instances where alteration in the language would diminish the power of the message.

On a personal note, I also experienced physical reactions during our writing sessions. Often, the reality of what Penney was saying would affect me so deeply that my fingers would freeze and I could not type. But, more commonly, my hands would fly across the keyboard, yet I did not fully comprehend many of the ideas until much later.

This is a healing handbook that has many levels. Although it is small in appearance, it is not a quick read. The wisdom and teachings presented through the words and artwork are those of a contemporary mystic and holy woman. This book offers instruction, clarity, answers, comfort and yet, above all, an energy that will work with you. You will be able to see something new in it each time you pick it up.

I still do.

Kathleen Spellman

PART I

HUMANITY

The Human Body
&
The Human Condition

Time and the Future:
Where We Are Headed

Pyramid of Being

"We evolved without clearing.
We forgot to heal and that is why we are so blocked
from our own evolution.
We need to go back and heal, then proceed."

The Human Body & the Human Condition

LIFE
Life beats…it breathes.
We begin.
True life is flow and passion that breathes.

The Body

The human being is in a structure, we are in a body. The body is part of Earth and it is our superficial connection to the Earth. It is our outer shell, it is what we appear to be.

The body gives us definition and mass and it makes us subject to physical laws, which in turn is part of our healing.

When we are in the body, there is also the element of time involved. This demands that patience be created.

As human beings, we are aware that our bodies can break. We need to be in a fragile form in order to be humble and vulnerable, and still know that we are powerful. We learn that our power exceeds the body.

The Body
The false gimmick
Imagery and confinement and the way the body looks have not received favorable attention.
The Body Picture

There is a negative rumor about the body…
What is the body worth?

Feelings

At times the human body feels like an unfavorable place to be. This occurs because of constriction, pain and false imagery. We should erase the many patterns of thought that have been taught to us about the limitations of what the body can and cannot do. We are meant to express, to feel, to be aware of the fact that the body has a beauty, and to use this body in a carefree manner. There exists a superficial human body that works and is meant to work in our favor. When this superficial body does not hold "issues," i.e. problems and worries, it can be flexible, pliable, and by all means beautiful.

When the body takes its presence on Earth it changes greatly with perspective. At times it is difficult to remain in this life, in our bodies. But, do we really wish to escape Earth? Maybe what we really want is to use the body as if it does not exist, merging and un-merging with it. We can fulfill our purpose and dreams through this system of the body, and have these dreams work for us here.

When people say, "I love the body, it feels good," they are experiencing feelings through the body. These feelings are not of the body. "Of the body" means the feelings are in the body. True feelings (passion, release, excitement and uncontrollable freedom) do not reside in the body. The body itself does not give us these feelings. Feelings of this type are deeper than the body and go beyond a structure.

When the body is filled with the goodness of what is close to our true spirit, it takes on a strength. It becomes resilient, preserved, large and beautiful. When the body is pure, when it is free, there is more of a connection to a limitless place and to Earth.

Beauty

False beauty, momentary beauty, or egotistical beauty is only skin-deep. When we love someone, looks do not matter. Without even realizing it, we may find ourselves attracted to others who bear similar physical characteristics to a person we have feelings of love for. We may even catch ourselves looking twice. "Is that the person I love? It looks so much like him (or her). I like that look." We feel a stirring inside. Often, what is actually unattractive to others becomes beauty in our eyes.

Beauty is what we make of it and it can change every day. True beauty is the summation of our positive and healed self. This beauty shines through because perfection does not exist.

"Beauty performs with itself and for itself.
It is an uncompromised range of our being."

Beauty is born from great knowing and under-standing.

The Essentials: Sleeping, Eating, Breathing

The concerns of Earth are the essentials: sleeping, eating, and breathing. Our instinctual power and our deep human nature know how to correct turmoil and bring our essentials back to balance. The body will always react when there is a dilemma. Sometimes the body needs an adjustment. Just as nature knows how to bring itself back to balance (back to center) so too does the human body.

When the body is going through a crisis, its homeostasis may also be in crisis. The human experience may be altered. We may have different patterns of sleeping, eating and breathing. When we try to eat the right way, try to exercise and observe the thought processes that run through our minds as we are going through these changes, the body will systematically take care of itself. When the body goes out of balance for a while, it is widening a gap so that more problems (issues) and blocks can be released. What's really happening is that healing is transpiring. Life is establishing itself in a meaningful way. After a purposeful restructuring, the body will take itself back to center and, once again, will attain its own rhythm.

Nutrition and Exercise

Nutrition and exercise are essential for growth. Any type of exercise will work when it is done properly.

Nutrition is our fuel and it may also be one of our

pleasures. It is significant. When we eat properly, we are able to maintain our resolve; our strength, both physical and mental, and our perspective.

Time and the Future: Where We Are Headed

"The Soul goes through many different episodes of growth. There really is no time."

We are in time to learn, and then to break out of it. On Earth, we are in a system of physics. We are in a sequence which creates timing. A sequence is like a beat, a vibration, a rhythm. It has intervals. Intervals create a timing that we use to establish balance.

Earth is in time. There is a link between the fact that we are here on Earth and that we are here in time.

"It is not always what it appears to be."

Humanity will break through this present-day sequence. Once humanity is altered, the vibration of Earth will become something new. Humility will be felt and balance will be established. The world powers will shift, and the world will come into its natural state.

Metamorphosis

The planet is going through a metamorphosis. It is shedding, and it is simultaneously re-emerging. It will be reborn. The Earth's "energy" is accelerated at this time. When catastrophic events take place, either naturally or man-made, they lead this planet into a new existence. This may be difficult to believe, especially when catastrophes are man-made. Once a deceitful, or even demonic, event transpires, the energy involved dies, is reborn, changes course and again becomes an opportunity for mankind.

We take on a predestined course. However, there is a part of this whole life process where there is freedom of choice. The predestined course can be altered if and when our choices change. From there a new plan is made, which then becomes the present predestined course.

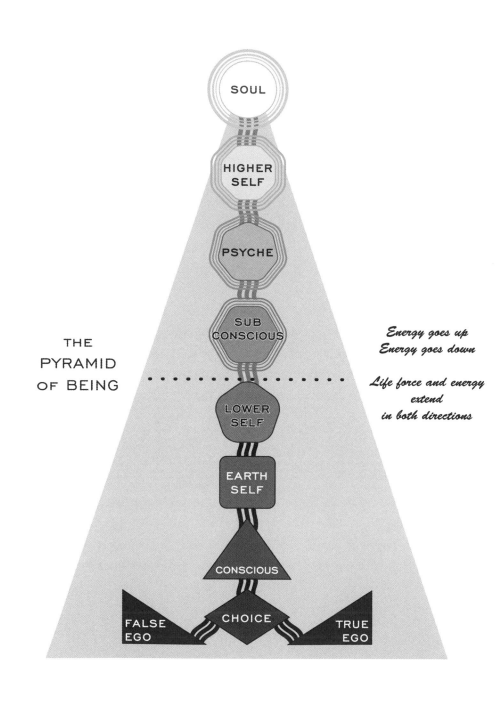

SOUL

HIGHER SELF

PSYCHE

SUB CONSCIOUS

LOWER SELF

EARTH SELF

CONSCIOUS

CHOICE

FALSE EGO

TRUE EGO

THE PYRAMID OF BEING

Energy goes up
Energy goes down

Life force and energy
extend
in both directions

"The soul goes through many different episodes of growth and also of just being."

Pyramid of Being

The diagram allows us to see a snapshot of ourselves as beings. We are not simple, we are not finite, and we are not confined to this Earth. We are universal. We are made up of energy and physicality. When energy shifts, the physicality shifts.

Soul : The immaterial essence, animating principle, or actuating cause of an individual life. The spiritual principle embodied in human beings, all rational and spiritual beings, or the universe. A person's total self.

The definition(s) in italics above are used by permission from Merriam-Webster Online Dictionary ©2004 by Merriam-Webster, Incorporated (www.Merriam-Webster.com).

The Soul is our piece/peace with God; our personal, prime connection to God.

The Higher Self is the true subconscious and the connection of the being to the soul. The higher self is our power source to God.
When we experience a higher guidance, a guardian angel on our shoulder, an inner voice, a spirit guide, this may be our *true guide*, our higher self in this vast world. *It is from here we get our unblocked answers.* The higher self knows.

The Psyche conducts the true ego (the pure earth self). It is the connection to the higher self.

Subconscious : The mental activities just below the threshold of consciousness.

The definition(s) in italics above are used by permission from Merriam-Webster Online Dictionary ©2004 by Merriam-Webster, Incorporated (www.Merriam-Webster.com).

The Subconscious is what we are not aware of.

The Lower Self, the Earth Self, the Ego, the Consciousness

This group has the freedom of choice. This is the structure of our being that shows itself here on Earth. It is what we are made up of in this physical realm.

The Ego is the structure that we need in order to be here and to be present on this planet.

Conscious : Perceiving, apprehending, or noticing with a degree of controlled thought or observation. Archaic : sharing another's knowledge or awareness of an inward state or outward fact.
Capable of or marked by thought, will, design, or perception.

The definition(s) in italics above are used by permission from Merriam-Webster Online Dictionary ©2004 by Merriam-Webster, Incorporated (www.Merriam-Webster.com).

The Consciousness is what we are aware of. The subconscious mixed with the consciousness is the conscience; that which tells us whether or not we are doing the right or wrong thing. It is from the conscience that we should make our choices. Choices are made from either the true or the false ego.

The False Ego is the lower, or earth self, that is living in denial, or under false pretenses. We may wander towards the wrong choices and then become egotistical about it.

The True Ego is the true way of living. It is what we should be and what we are striving to be. The true ego is our structure here when we become whole and present with ourselves.

Universe

Each of us has our own universe which is comprised of our hopes, aspirations, our memories, our ideas and ideals, and the factual knowledge of what exists for us in our world. In life we set up our world and our universe to use for our higher command – to bring us home, to bring us to our power and to our soul. Our universes work with the universe and this universe works for and with us. It is at our disposal and so is this Earth.

The universe is the ever-ending and beginning flow of universal energy. The universe knows what we need, what we must have and what we will truly enjoy. A system of balance provides a current of action and energy that will move and merge with itself as it carries out life.

Each universe interacts within the others to set a plan in motion. This system is put into action by a higher source. This higher source is protected by God and is made up of our own piece of God.

HEALING

Life will supply us with the healing road
that is necessary.
We do not have to seek out healing.
It is happening to us all the time.
We can deny it – but not forever,
because the ego is not in charge of our healing.
Healing comes from a higher source within us.

CHAPTER 2

Healing
Healers
&
Karma

Why Now?

"Truth, life and essence are always salvageable.
They will always come to light,
but it is about how much struggle we will go through
to get there."

Healing

Heal : To make sound or whole: to restore to health. To cause (an undesirable condition) to be overcome. To restore to original purity or integrity. To return to a sound state.

The definition(s) in italics above are used by permission from Merriam-Webster Online Dictionary ©2004 by Merriam-Webster, Incorporated (www.Merriam-Webster.com).

"True healing is the ability to see through the façade; the ability for the body and the mind to be comfortable and peaceful. True healing is to feel free."

"The body knows how to heal itself no matter what."

Healing is a unique venture. It is an expression that we want to become responsible, to thrive, to be creative and whole.

Healing means our life is different. It is discovering our gifts.

When people say they want to "heal," the range of what this means can be very broad; physical, mental, emotional, spiritual or any combination of these.

"How do I recognize myself? Become myself? Become unafraid? Become happy? How do I see truth? Why do I suffer?"

To discover these answers is the journey known as healing.

All human beings want to be healed. We all take different routes to obtain this, but our path brings us to the same destination. We are all headed for the same place, wholeness with ourselves. Healing will allow each of us to enjoy life distinctly and uniquely.

There are several ways to view healing. The word healing has acquired a stigma.

There are people who feel that healing cannot fit comfortably within a lifestyle and do not want to look at any of the aspects involved. They may think it is silly, they do not believe that it exists, or they just don't have time for it; it may seem overwhelming. "It will attach itself to me and I won't be able to get rid of it." "It will get in the way of my lifestyle." "My life now is just the way life is, and I'll deal with it." There is no basis for this reasoning.

Others feel that to admit they need to heal is to admit that they are deficient. "If I have to heal, I am not right. Something is wrong with me." This can be overwhelming. Healing is a part of us. It is not all of what we are about.

Conversely, there are also people who may *use* healing everyday. It is very much a part of their life and they do not want to give it up. When people exploit healing to suit their lifestyle, they are using it to justify holding on to their self-neediness. "I'm healing so leave me alone." They count on the journey of healing to serve them; a purpose in their life – and they use it as a crutch. In this case, healing takes the direction of codependency. Healing has nothing to do with codependency.

These assorted views of healing are misleading. So then what really is "healing" and how can we begin to understand the role it plays in our lives?

Healing is a natural, finite process not meant to take over our lives but to free us to live more fully.

Somewhere in our being we have all acquired energetic patterns and experiences that filter through us in positive and negative ways.

The negative patterning, negative energy, false feelings and pain accumulate within our system, but they cannot be assimilated because they are not part of who we truly are. This "dis-ease," or disruption, needs to be cleared and healed because it will only cause friction, denial and true defeat wherever we go.

But, when positive energy, patterning, circumstances and joyful feelings are experienced and brought into our being, we do integrate and blend with them. They aid in our development because they *are* a part of who we are.

Healing is trusting that when we want something to take place – it *will*. Healing will not take anything away from us that we need or truly desire.

"Everybody's feelings get hurt.
Everybody is sensitive – it just got twisted somewhere."

Healing just wants to happen. We have *all* come here broken in some way. Healing is essential so that life can become essential.

When we are involved in the act of healing, we are naturally protected. Protection is purity; they surround and fortify each other.

"Darkness can not stick to purity.
It does not run as deep as purity does."

Healing is Finite

As human beings, we often hold on to stress, illness, pain or any issue that causes us discomfort because we do not think there is an alternative, a solution. We set ourselves up to believe that distress and suffering are normal parts of life and somehow we will get through it. We confuse being healed with getting by. Getting by is getting by. It is not the same as thriving, it is not open-ended.

Feeling ill is not wrong:
- Sometimes the body is discharging a toxic element. This element can be held in our body, psyche or in our emotional spirit. In this case, illness is discharging illness.

- It is the body's way of bringing up an issue or a pattern that needs to be recognized, so it can *then* be healed.
- Illness always works within a deeper paradigm.

Being healed is to understand stress – stress with work, with money, with health, with relationships – all issues that cause stress. Stress is trying to get our attention. Or it may be eliminating something that is inside of us. These issues vibrate within us, causing deep pain, sometimes over and over again.

Once we understand the issues, we can break them apart and learn from them. We discharge the bad; assimilate the good and then move on.

Healing will not go on forever.

The Healing Process

The Healing of One
Ask for help when necessary.
Don't suppose,
Don't lean,
Don't compromise
and
Don't give up.

"Perspective and perception; the building blocks of the mind."

The body, the mind, and the soul heal themselves. The healing process is meant to take place inside of us. It is an organic and easily accessed system of discharging, reuniting and receiving. Healing should not be sensationalized.

Healing does not have to occur in a linear process. It moves in waves, and then it is at rest. It comes in pieces, and then makes breakthroughs.

Healers

Healing itself is not supposed to be a business. It is a give-and-take between healer and client. Neither one is supreme. When healers feel they have control, or an advantage over another person or situation, the results they are trying to obtain will go awry. First of all, this is because one person, the healer, is trying to dominate another, the client. And secondly, the client is submitting or relinquishing his or her true power to another. Nothing but egotistical fanfare is accomplished.

"A healer is anyone who creates anything to be whole."

Healers are found in every walk of life and can range from the professional you seek out to the chance meeting of someone on the street.

A healer, or a person with pure intent who has a gift, most likely never sought it out. They possess an opening of insight. Humility engenders a deeper connection with God and facilitates a healer's ability to move energy beyond where it is. Healers, when healing, have given up control.

When an issue is ready to break through, any healer, with compassion and empathy, can cause that moment to happen. Any type of humbleness stimulates change. Change heals.

We can apply this to all areas of healing in our life, whether physical, emotional or spiritual.

"Be careful to be led and not to conquer
or be conquered."

The action of healing should come from deep inside of oneself. When it feels like someone is manipulating or overtaking us and not respecting us as individuals or equals, this is wrong. We need to separate ourselves from these situations and re-evaluate.

Alternately, when a detoxification, discharge or release is happening through the body, mind or soul, it may not feel good; but given some time, deep inside we will know it is right. The process itself is significant and needs to happen. Even though it may hurt for a while, it is important to ride with it because issues, problems and pain are clearing. After a given amount of time, if changes or results are not (or are no longer) apparent, we need to seek help again.

To the healer: Separate and the precise action will transpire.

"Resistance may be for a good reason.
If you feel pressured, circumstances may not be right
for now, or for always."

Karma

Karma is very much a part of the healing process.

Karma is the accumulation of the positive and negative deeds and patterns which have been produced over time and have settled in the soul. It is the shopping list of what we want to work out, get rid of and/or use to our advantage while we are on this earth. Karma may be so direct that it addresses itself in one dramatic surge; or it can be slow and subtle, playing itself out over time.

"Karma is the beginning… the solution is the end."

In the past, we may have encountered stumbling blocks and consequences due to ignorance and out of denial. We want to feel what we have done wrong and where we have been held back so we can literally learn through our mistakes. The karmic path brings patterns into their truth.

At times the people who move in and out of our lives are also part of our karma. Some trigger deep responses. Old relationships may resurface; new ones will come in and then vanish just as rapidly as they appeared. These people may not stay in our circle, but whoever they are, they are perfect for what we are learning at this particular stage of our life. They may be people we have old karma with, or people who mirror the very issues we are letting go of.

Karma is not a punishment. There is good karma and there is bad karma. We will work through the bad karma. The good karma will never leave us – we have succeeded.

Procrastination & Decision-making

"Accomplishment is the essence of the human delivery."

Procrastination plays the biggest part in why this world is not healed. Procrastination equals denial.

Procrastination can generate a lack of decision-making or hasty decision-making. Decision-making is an art and an important part of coming through procrastination. We procrastinate at times because we are afraid that we cannot make the right decision. We may also want to believe we are on a correct path, so we *create* a path by making a decision before the path is revealed to us. A decision in itself has nothing to do with the manner in which the conclusion, or outcome, will be formed. Our higher power can supersede any decision. Situations and answers may change according to whatever purpose, or truths, are involved. Decisions are an inroad to the truth, but we are not able to figure out that truth from the decision. A decision unravels into a destiny. But the destiny is not a *controlled* part of the decision.

When we make any decision, an energy inside of us literally shifts into a direction. Wanting the right outcome for our higher good will prompt the energy to give a clear result. Once our intent for the right answer is there, we should proceed forward. We will quickly be shown if that decision was wrong. At this point, it should be easy to rectify and change the situation because humility and surrender were attached to the original decision. An unobstructed, non-manipulated decision eliminates procrastination and we are then able to move forward.

While we are on a healing path, old obstacles may come up through the decisions we make. This is not to be feared for it is a natural part of healing. The more we initiate decision-making, the more artful at it we will become and solutions will be revealed sooner rather than later.

"Help! I'm smart, but I'm not good at anything."

Laziness

No one is *born* lazy. We are born fearful, which can paralyze us, keeping us from forward motion until we are willing to face the fear and open a roadway to resolution. Or, we are born with an ego that does not want to change, does not want to give up or that does not want to get in the race. The ego stays at the same beat so we stay dulled-out. Dullness equals laziness.

"Don't feel disgraced. You can start anywhere."

Denial

Denial occurs when a person does not want to *see* clearly. It is an act of the false ego. Denial serves no purpose.

However, the term denial is used too frequently as a catchall for what may be a more complicated reasoning as to why healing is not carried out. For example, denial is often inadvertently substituted when a "natural depression" is taking place. A natural depression is the means by which the subconscious slows down a growth process (which *is* useful and often necessary). This natural depression is blocking, and hence protecting our mind's active way of thinking. The issue (whatever it is) may be too much for the mind to absorb all at once. This purposeful slowing-down may indicate that we are waiting for the right moment, or event, to catalyze healing. The depression acts like a valve that has not yet been opened, and the subconscious is keeping the flow in order.

Freedom vs. Consistency

We need to be totally free, and we need consistency to feel secure.

Consistency is a settling in. It is a knowing that things are safe, that atmospheres and people are safe and that our instincts are correct and can be counted on. It is the act of being nurtured.

Freedom allows us to feel that there are no strings attached, there is a clear horizon, that we can always pursue what we wish for and what we want and that, ultimately, nothing can hold us back.

We all need this dance between feeling safe and feeling limitless.

Why Now?

Healing cannot be negotiated and it cannot be ignored. The world is changing quickly, and the use of the world's power is shifting. At this time in our history, we are also changing dramatically. The entire world is in an agitated state, which makes for an ideal space for healing to take place. It is fertile ground.

We are coming into a psychic world, a spiritual world. Psychic action is a form of spirituality. People wrongly associate psychic ability with sensationalism, which it is not. "Psychic" is when our senses, our eyes, our body, our ears, are able to see where our human eyes cannot. When we add this to the substance of the human experience, we will go forward in a way that we have previously only dreamed about.

Psychic ability is tricky and it needs to step out of its own way to be useful.

Spiritual healing is at the root of any physical or emotional healing. When each person is truly healed spiritually, they have trust in themselves and they are *in* trust with higher power – it works both ways.

To date, there has been a separation between healing and what this world is about. There is a strong barrier between living a regular life, and living a healed life. Why is this?

There is a frenetic current running through the world which makes us feel anxious about the smallest things. The world is in a disoriented place with itself. We may also feel such frantic feelings coming through us. This is the world's emotion attaching to our own.

Interesting and unusual illnesses are manifesting within all cultures so that we will look deeper within ourselves, where we have not looked before. A certain humbleness will be the end result. In dealing with crisis, we should not be confused or worried. Once the inner part of our being is healed, it will project out into all situations of the world.

In the future, the world will come into its own to re-evaluate, reorganize, redistribute, reform and reunite. We will become *whole* because we are meant to survive. This is more about individual healing than it is about forcing a healing onto something other than oneself. The Earth will clear when we clear. Healing is always about an individual experience.

PART II

THE IDEAS OF
HEALING

"Intent is our most valuable tool."

CHAPTER 3

Spirituality

"Spirituality is a state of grace.
It is the force of God through this
imperfect world.
It is the truth without the mask."

Spirituality

Spirituality : Sensitivity or attachment to religious values. The quality or state of being spiritual.

Spiritual : Of, relating to, consisting of, or affecting the spirit: incorporeal. Of or relating to sacred matters. Concerned with religious values. Related or joined in spirit.

Religion : The service and worship of God or the supernatural. Commitment or devotion to religious faith or observance. A personal set or institutionalized system of religious attitudes, beliefs, and practices. A cause, principle, or system of beliefs held to with ardor and faith.

The definition(s) in italics above are used by permission from Merriam-Webster Online Dictionary ©2004 by Merriam-Webster, Incorporated (www.Merriam-Webster.com).

"We all have a different way of looking at things.
Everyone's spirituality may be different, also.
Forthright action speaks for itself
with no agenda necessary."

Spirituality is what religion should have been – and will be again.

Spirituality is expansion. Spirituality soars above what is proper, what is in order, critical, scary or judgmental. It changes within each human being to serve their purpose, and, yet, spirituality is pure and untouched. Each person has his or her own unique rhythm. That is what makes us separate. Spirituality takes this into account, always.

Spirituality is solace in the raging storm of perplexity and doubt. It is the cyclone of goodness that surrounds despair, hopelessness, fanatical behavior and doom. Spirituality projects itself and leads us through any debilitating phase that we must endure during our lifespan. It is a living force that has compassion.

Spirituality is a feeling that we have *with* God, a freedom. It is divine intervention.

The subject of spirituality is often too broad for us to grasp. We may feel that the concepts of God and spirituality are incomprehensible and, therefore, out of reach. In the true reality, they are the deepest and most accessible areas of our lives. Regardless of whether we break the ideas of God and spirituality apart, or keep them whole, they are both simple and completely unthreatening. They are vast and perfect enough to serve a purpose away from this world; and, yet, soothing enough to give us total comfort at any moment.

When we take religion away from our belief system, we may feel that we are left with nothing; we are left without structure. However, when religious beliefs are threatening, or carry a critical edge, judgment takes place. Only God has the right to put things in order. Spirituality will outlive set religions because it does not hold onto control; it is not locked into a belief system. Spirituality is a free fall. It is not a doctrine. The consequences of wrong decisions, dilemmas or any kind of trauma are intended, ultimately, to lead us back to God.

Spirituality has no criteria. It loves to give praise.

It congratulates anything that is working in a pure way. Spirituality carries no guilt.

"I believe that every great leader was placed here,
or put him or herself here,
to put forth knowledge and then step aside;
to let each man find his own faith within himself."

There is a higher reasoning here and we need to trust and accept that this is so.

Energy interweaves in a way we cannot perceive. The mind tries to control. The mind is linear, and is unable to distinguish what is actually happening. Our connection with God always functions at a much higher level than what we experience physically on Earth.

No one can sever another person's connection with God. Each connection is divine, holy and sacred.

CHAPTER 4

Issues & Process

"When we heal,
there is a direct connection to a focal point.
There are many situations in life
which are also attached to this focal point.
Once the core issue is released,
the struggles that have been associated with the issue
will fade away."

Issues

Issue : The action of going, coming, or flowing out. A final outcome that usually constitutes a solution (as of a problem) or resolution (as of a difficulty). A vital or unsettled matter. The point at which an unsettled matter is ready for a decision...

The definition(s) in italics above are used by permission from Merriam-Webster Online Dictionary ©2004 by Merriam-Webster, Incorporated (www.Merriam-Webster.com).

The issues that we carry with us through life are the heaviest burdens of this world. However, we do possess within us the means to discharge them through what is called process.

This chapter has to do with results. It is perhaps the most crucial in explaining how the healing within us happens. We examine what we need to be aware of, and how to step out of our own way to facilitate healing on all levels. We learn what issues are and how to let go of them (or to enable them to let go of us) for all time.

When a thought, an element or an incident disrupts our life, or otherwise creates havoc or points itself out, it is an issue that is setting itself in order to prepare to change. Our external life is reflecting an internal struggle. The body and/or emotional field are exposing and bringing forward the pain and discomfort that need to be healed.

An issue is a situation or a pattern that stands in our way of becoming whole, of finding peace. Examples of issues are fear, addiction, obsession, shame, guilt, envy, anger, codependency and depression. It is something that is bigger than it should be and it hurts.

"Issues are hell."

Our issues come forward only when we are strong enough to confront them. In order for an issue to surface for healing, we need to be somewhat clear around the situation that the issue is pertaining to, even if that clarity is subconscious. When we feel that a disruption is occurring, it is a sign that we are awakening. The universe and our higher self are at work.

When we bring an issue into acknowledgement, we bring it into light. We are releasing it because we are not afraid to see it, to state it or to live with it and to let go of the pain it has caused. When it is recognized fully, it has no more strength. We see things differently. We are clear.

Patterns, old traumas, reactions to people and events are all carried within the body, the psyche and sometimes even the soul. When these elements are traumatic, they cause pain. Deeply held negative situations and patterns will find ways to express themselves through *anything* in our existence, at *any time*. We begin to notice our issues and old feelings revealing themselves in all parts of our life. They can be found in current events, in the people around us, in our own moods and in the world at large. It may look like we are embracing these situations because they are all around us – but the fact is that we are ready to discharge them for good, and that is why they keep re-presenting themselves to us.

We set up relationships within our world to mirror our deeply held pain, trauma and issues. While we discharge an issue we *vibrate* alongside it. The issue, *now* through move-ment, parallels itself through our life as it comes forward and releases.

Every issue carries a vibration. Once we understand and release one problem, all situations and thought pro-cesses attached to that vibration and problem will dissipate. Conversely, if we choose to hold onto an issue, almost every-thing we do in our daily life will reflect that issue to varying degrees. It may come up in a range of situations at times, but it will always bring up the same fear, tension or other unsettled negative feelings in the same way.

"All things in life are a reflection of what we have inside us and show us where we need to go."

A Perplexed Relationship with Ourselves & Others

When we are hurt and a fractured aspect of ourselves surfaces, we act out. For a time, it may seem that we actu-ally become that wounded part. We wonder how a person, or ourselves, could change so dramatically in such a quick period of time. "Who is that person?" "Who am I?" This is an issue exhibiting itself. The issue itself is so unlike who we truly are that it occupies a bigger percentage of us (or it appears to) because it is so abstract. The more this personality, or characteristic, is *not* like us, the more it appears to be an obstacle. This "issued" piece is so inappropriate it looms forward.

When an issue or issues are fully on display and there is no recognition that a problem dwells within (when denial precedes healing), the human will work against his or her true self.

An issue that is locked into our psyche, spirit, emotional field or body will pre-empt any form of, or devotion to, love. In other words, when the soul is compromised and the ego does not choose to get out of its own way, even love cannot be felt with wholeness or with purity. In this case, the energy of one's own being is constantly used to reinforce the ego of the issue. In turn, this sacrifices love, or balance, with any other human being or with life.

A relationship where two people are on two different paths of existence (one on the path of healing and the other on the path of denial) cannot be maintained. When our lives are invested in other lives that carry issue-laden identity, the relationships will only result in abandonment, misunderstanding and loneliness.

When an issue shifts, is shed or is integrated properly, many situations in our lives change and the negative personality aspects rooted within this issue are healed. A string of events will follow to enable this to happen.

Discharge and Detoxification

Discharge : To relieve of a charge, load, or burden. To release from an obligation. To release from confinement, custody, or care. To give outlet or vent to.

Detoxify : To remove a poison or toxin or the effect of such from. To render (a harmful substance) harmless.

The definition(s) in italics above are used by permission from Merriam-Webster Online Dictionary ©2004 by Merriam-Webster, Incorporated (www.Merriam-Webster.com).

"Pain is a transmission to get to something else."

"Physicality knows its own discharge."

In healing, the principles of discharge and detox apply to the entire being, whether physical, emotional or spiritual. When we discharge, we let go of an issue of false belief. We release old patterns. The detox is a release of the poisons connected to the issue and patterns, emotionally (feelings), physically (mind and body) and/or spiritually (the soul). As we discharge the issue, we are simultaneously getting rid of all of the toxins associated with it.

Emotional discharges vary. Fear can release through tears, shaking, or trembling; anger through temper tantrums; even the fitful, sleepless nights we experience may be a detox. We discharge and detox in many ways that are often overzealous, usually in an overt manner. Although these actions serve us, they may feel painful for a time.

Physical and mental illness are the discharge and detox

of the body/mind. Rashes, aches, pains, fractured bones and disease are various manifestations of illness that the body employs to release issues or to allow us to become aware of them. We are then prompted and able to facilitate the process. A mental discharge, or recognition of an issue, may present itself as an unpleasant or repetitive thought that lies heavy on our minds through obsession, guilt or anger. It bites at us constantly, so it is releasing by obsessing. The body not only knows how to heal itself, it knows how to bring attention to disharmony in itself.

The spirit is our deepest level. The discharge or detox may be so potent or so extreme that it may necessitate a *break-down/breakthrough* or what is called a *dark night of the soul*. When the soul wants to heal, sometimes the trauma that we experience can be quite intense, but the reward is well worth the time, effort and sacrifice.

Direction

When an understanding becomes clear, or a positive revelation occurs to us, any clarity that eases the conscience – I am worthwhile, I have courage, I am beautiful – nurtures and fosters a forward motion. This motion will go further. We proceed with positive reinforcement.

On the other hand, when a negative understanding that has held us back is revealed, such as an issue (alcohol addiction, compulsive gambling, jealousy etc.), it is coming forward because it wants to be altered. By recognizing it, we address it, and it can transform.

We work with the positive aspects of our lives, or we begin to transform the negative. In both cases, we are in a win-win situation. Clarity directs us.

Process

Process : A natural phenomenon marked by gradual changes that lead toward a particular result (the process of growth). A natural continuing activity or function (such life processes as breathing). A series of actions or operations conducing to an end.

The definition(s) in italics above are used by permission from Merriam-Webster Online Dictionary ©2004 by Merriam-Webster, Incorporated (www.Merriam-Webster.com).

"Process is time."

We go through process at all turns in our lives. Some are easy processes and some are challenging. Challenging processes bring us to the easy ones. This chapter speaks of process regarding issues – which, for the most part, are those processes seen as challenging. We grow and learn through both. The learning is more exact and crucial during our challenging times. However, when we reach the point of easy, or positive process, we are usually issue-free. This is called living.

While we are healing, a process is always underway.

Process is the procedure that we go through to release the issue.

When we comprehend and are able to feel the fear around an issue, the root of the problem can be resolved and dissolved.

We usually go through a *subconscious process* before it becomes conscious. During this time we may feel disoriented, lethargic, on edge, worried, angry, fearful, guilty, etc. for no apparent reason. Then the more obvious, *conscious process* will become available to us. The conscious process may begin with a personal failure or success, an illness or healing, a severing or a beginning of a relationship, a change in residence, the emergence of a phobia, etc. Conscious process could also involve a thought that brings us into an awareness about ourselves, or a situation that needs to change. These are all doorways to process. At times it will seem like there is no direction, no order to this. This is normal and it is essential that this part of process play itself out.

Moving Through It

There are times in our lives when we feel we are victims, or that we are being punished for some unknown reason. When negative situations arise, they are not unkind or harsh acts that are being committed upon us. We are never being punished. In order to change, to release outmoded patterning, we have decided to bring an unresolved problem, or deep burden, to conclusion. As a result of this negative situation, we are caught in confusion. This causes us to let go of our desire to create an outcome. Patterns of control will ease, loosen, and our power will be fortified and will emerge. A path will open and reveal truth. We will use this path to help push forward and out all accumulated pain, guilt, fear, abandonment, greed, etc. We are left with who we really are.

An issue has not been fully transformed until we thoroughly feel comforted by the release of pain. We forget about our pain, and we are able to proceed with life, without pain.

"The issue and the process are bringing us into the glorious state of humility and patience – which is necessary for anything to proceed on this Earth."

So, how do we move through process?

At some point during a process, we are called upon to take responsibility; to face an issue directly. Taking responsibility means to become fully aware of and acknowledging an issue. "I am uncomfortable." "I hurt." " I have hurt myself or someone else." " Someone has hurt me." " I may not even know why it is that it hurts." "I admit this is affecting me." "It feels wrong." When we allow higher influences (the conscience, intuition, or time) to lead us, answers *will* be given. New direction comes into our lives when we follow what is presented to us day-by-day. The pain will continue to move through, and we will become clear.

Whether a pain is physical, emotional or spiritual, if our approach is humble, and we make necessary adjustments in our lives to respect change and recognition, a healing will take place. If we are doing all we can to deal with the issue without controlling expectations, focusing or fixating on an outcome, we will start to feel that movement is, indeed, occurring. When we are having trouble being patient during a process, we must sustain our humility within our search for an answer. The problem, issue, or dilemma, may be working itself out as best as it can, even if it is not apparent.

*"The reward for our patience is healing wounds
from so long ago."*

The Universe With Process

When we feel pain, the universe, in order to aid in the healing, usually works in reverse. In other words, it bombards us with a negative slant, stumbling blocks or overt signs that something is wrong. This happens so that deep inside we reach out for an answer. We need to feel the full extent of the situation and what the situation has done to us in the past. Knowing this, we will then shift the situation at the very foundation where it was created.

*"I am doing everything right,
why is everything going wrong?"*

There are two reasons we are not given the positive

side of a healing. First, we would never change or seek an-swers if our life just rolled along. Second, the pain, the hurt and the fear have to be "matched," or paralleled, to be released and resolved. It is the only way life can come to terms with itself. So through our struggle, thoughts, actions and con-victions, we focus on that part of us that needs attention. We look inside ourselves for answers with renewed energy from a reserve because we "do not want to take this anymore." It is not that we must always learn through struggle, but while strong shifts are occurring, the challenges presented enable us to go deeper.

Recognizing the presence of our pain is essential. We should not feel the need to state or live with the feeling of positive reinforcement as a mantra or as a daily reminder that everything is all right, when it is not true. "I am whole, I am happy, and my being is above it all." That is using false positive reinforcement, out of fear, to persuade ourselves into believing that we have (prematurely) achieved wholeness.

Positive reinforcement should seek a resolution. "I want to be happy, I want to have peace, I do not want to have this pain anymore." By stating an *expectation* of positive results, we honor where we are *now*. When we profess that everything is all right, we are not living in the moment of the pain. We are ignoring the fact that we can heal in the moment.

"It is the presence of the moment
that will deliver the solution."

Also, if necessary, do not be afraid to live "in between" the problem and the answer. At every point of process, there is value and learning.

There is more than just this world. What we experience here on Earth is in the moment and temporary. But, when we do not acknowledge that we are presently in pain, we step into an answer before it is given. Positive reinforcement is important and worthwhile. It helps us to set our sights and goals into the future. If it is fear that taints our relationship with pain, then the pain becomes larger than what it really is. To admit that we hurt is the beginning of our way out of the pain.

Patterns

An issue is a result of a *pattern*. It can be presented through a pattern, or it is the reason we formulated a pattern. A pattern, in this case, is a sequence of false energy that works through us but which does not reflect who we really are. When issues or patterns are held in our body, they become part of the fabric out of which we are made.

A negative pattern may be a habit that needs to be broken. Even after we've broken it, the pattern surrounding the habit or behavior may persist for a while – until it, too, breaks apart. As the pattern slows down, it dissipates. This may sound abstract, but the pattern literally has to vibrate out of our energetic field. It took time to create it. A cycle, or a measure of time, has to take place because *we* are in a measure of time. The duration of the cycle may vary depending upon how deeply the pattern is intertwined with the core of our being.

There is also the possibility that, without even realizing it, we have been working on a particular issue, and any karma associated with the issue, for a long period of time. We have, in effect, already gone through a cycle of release. By the time we become consciously aware of our efforts, we are near a solution.

If we have carried an issue/pattern for a long time within our soul, or within our psyche, the issue behaves and proceeds at the same energetic current (frequency) as when it originally transpired. A current that portrays what has happened in the past is established. It feels the same because it *is* the same. By facing the problem once more, we have the opportunity to discharge it as it is repeated. We have a chance to eliminate the issue permanently.

The Importance of Time With Process, Issues and the World

An issue causes a fracture within us. When the issue is departing from the atmosphere within our world, we set up the groundwork for an unsettled period of time. We are creating a fractured opening for this fractured piece. We may feel distress while we are releasing the issue. This distress may alter time. Time may seem to move quickly, it may seem to slow down. *Something* that does not fit has to come through an unfit opening. Detoxification and discharge can now take place.

The world is in a subjective system of timing. So when this world is uncomfortable, our timing is uncomfortable. But, when our world runs smoothly along and we are issue-free, our time is in balance and we feel comfortable even when we are learning. This learning is direct. It is not buried deep inside of us, hidden amongst issues. It is a clean learning experience, we learn moment by moment.

An issue may leave directly or it may create a lesson while it is processing through. The element of time has its own learning properties attached to it. The pain and the process of healing wounds from the past are not linear, but the feelings associated with that issue are always the same, until we discharge them. Once we are finished healing, our timing will be individual and in sync with the world.

Process with Illness

"Physicality is only a release."

Part of the process in becoming who we really are is often to take on, and work through, physical and mindful disorders. In order to release or bring attention to itself, an issue will usually go to the weakest and/or the strongest area of the body or the mind. It will use a part of the body or mind that it has used before.

An illness may be trying to tell us that some part of our lives need to be changed; or, sometimes, it is creating that change for us. When our minds are occupied with worry or stress; when our bodies fracture, get digestive disorders, have respiratory problems or go into any type of dis-ease, we are healing. In any of these cases a *disruption* has reached the last level of our being, the body, and is coming through to bring about change and to heal. This will start a process, a string of occurrences intended to keep pushing the issue through.

An illness provides cleansing in conjunction with new circumstances and new avenues of thought. Once we look at our illness as a road sign directing us, or as a discharge, and not as a catastrophe, misfortune or setback that is happening *to us*, the illness then becomes a signal for new direction. We should not blame ourselves. The illness is a tool we are using to obtain wholeness with our spirit.

When psychic or emotional energies accumulate, the body may block, or armor itself against what is happening. This may create uncomfortable feelings. The body may resist the exit of energy for a while because there is too much to come through at once. It will literally bear down and tighten up. We may experience this as physical pain in the area we are releasing from. This is part of the natural sequence of healing. The energy will come through. Give it time.

When we feel lost, confused, even physically ill, and we do not know where this is leading us, it is a good sign that we are not trying to control a process. Even depression serves its function here. Depression has a place in keeping rage, or locked fear, dormant while we are in stages of reinstating ourselves.

"Confusion can be seen as a state of co-fusion, bringing together old and new to create something completely fresh."

The issues that we are releasing often appear at particularly inconvenient times. This works in our favor because the energy of the body has opened for change. Our defenses are down. Changes will happen, one after another. We become more aware at this point. Healing can take place more quickly. We may feel overwhelmed, but at the same time, we will be given whatever we need to continue.

"I love change except where I don't like it."

Dark Night of the Soul – the Super Issue

The term "dark night of the soul" is used to describe a devastating feeling, an overwhelming sensation that we ourselves, and/or everything in our lives, is wrong. This trauma usually takes place at an accentuated point of time. We should recognize that this is an important aspect of our lives and there is no reason to fear the *darkest* part of this ordeal.

The dark night of the soul is an exaggerated issue in process. It is not glamorous. It is *the* issue that causes us to toss and turn and spend all *night* consumed with our discomfort. No answers are available. We wrestle in pain with the conflict, or in confusion because the trial within becomes so heavy and so burdensome that we literally do not know what to do with ourselves.

The dark night of the soul is a metaphor for ridding ourselves of an issue that has become exposed on the deepest level of who we are. Our spirit clashes with our heaviest human fear. The dark night of the soul is personal to each of us, taking us to where our issue has been buried. Our fear may be strong, but our soul knows how to contain and utilize this fear in a safe and healing way. This, in turn, allows healing energy to parallel the fear, which brings us into the light. Everything we experience during this time period is essential and purposeful. We are subconsciously in control as we release the lid from our deepest demon.

"The darkness has to be met with the same amount of light
if it is to shake the ground it was built on,
to transmute it back to light. And through this struggle, we
build a foundation of deep truth within."

The dark night always breaks through to the light of day. It is important to stay steady within this period of time as much as possible, and to just *be*. The timing involved depends upon the magnitude of darkness that is working itself through us. We may need to actively participate as the issue wrestles with itself to come through us. In doing so, we become active in the delivery of an answer. All this will be shown. Once that day breaks, there will be a solution – regardless of whether the answer is active or passive. It will change.

"Process knows its course.
It is in sync with time.
It cannot be hurried.
It is a service offered that we take to reach an end."

A Reason People Do Not Go Into a Process

When we do not go into process, or we block the process from taking a natural course, it is because of fear.

One of our worst fears is that we will feel a distur-bance surface from deep inside, and there will be no one there with whom we can share it. Or, that when we feel the pain, other people whom we trust will be skeptical, confused or will just not believe us. The incredible weight of carrying pain without recognition can be almost too much to bear. It becomes debilitating to us. We think, "I must be wrong, no one else sees this." We can become angry and panicked, or may become numb; we close up and shut down.

Another reason we do not go into process is based on the fear that *it* will alter our lifestyle, we will never be finished with it and we do not have the time for it. If we want answers from an ego-based position, we may ignore process.

We find ways to work around what life wants to provide for us naturally, so we create our own answers. When they are not the right answers, we become frustrated and feel like we are losing, or that there are no answers. We waste more energy and time circumventing the problem, and avoiding a healing, than if we had just confronted it in the first place. Our life continues and we continue, still broken and feeling stuck. We put ourselves at a disadvantage because we feel that this is the way it is, when in reality, *anything* can be healed.

Once we allow ourselves to feel comfortable with total discomfort, recognition will surface and healing becomes purposeful. If it is there, it is there for a reason. When we shed an issue, the relief and the joy that we experience is unsurpassed.

It is very important not to judge the changes and challenges during healing times. Any feelings that surface (rage, fear, hopelessness) are acceptable. Respect the feelings, and know that they will not stay. Feelings move and shift much more easily than we imagine. Do not try to push them away or block their release. It is crucial to allow old buried feelings to come up and out; it is one of the most vital parts of the process.

Again, the initial traumas that created these feelings ages ago must be matched in some way, literally or symbolically, in order to allow the release. The closer the feelings rise to the surface, the more intense they can become. Just let it all happen.

"We usually feel the issue the most
when it is leaving us forever."

Keep in Mind…

At times during the process we need to be alone. This protects the rawness and the vulnerability of some of the spaces that we are opening to, both physical and nonphysical. At other times, it can be useful to be with people who are going through a healing process themselves.

We will *always* find an answer to an issue, a problem or anything that is uncomfortable or causes despair.

Unless:
- The ego gets in the way, and somehow or other we think it serves us to hold onto the problem – a form of codependency.
- We are still learning lessons through the issue, and our stages of development are not yet finished. This will conclude.
- We are performing a mission. We are giving up our self and our time to clarify a situation, event or dilemma that is not ours in order to help others see and heal. This is a passion that lies deep within us that we may not even be aware of, a sacrifice of the soul. It knows when its journey is finished.

We are always attached to the past if there is an uneasiness and lack of peace in our soul. This burden is carried with us until it is discharged. When an answer is ready to be received, an issue is ready to be healed; then we go back for it, heal it – and that is where we started.

The Ego:

True & False

Pitfalls of the Ego:

Greed, Guilt, Shame

"When do I feel safe?"

The Ego: True & False

Ego : The self especially as contrasted with another self or the world. The one of the three divisions of the psyche in psychoanalytic theory that serves as the organized conscious mediator between the person and reality especially by functioning both in the perception of and adaptation to reality.

The definition(s) in italics above are used by permission from Merriam-Webster Online Dictionary ©2004 by Merriam-Webster, Incorporated (www.Merriam-Webster.com).

From the Ancient Greeks to modern psychiatry, the concept of "ego" has been discussed for centuries. The scientific or technical definition of ego is very different from the more common interpretation of the term, which is used too often to describe those who are considered to be self-centered, pompous or full of themselves. "What an ego!" "He's so egotistical."

So what really is the ego and why is it so important in healing?

Understanding this concept is akin to looking deeply into a mirror. For many of us, it may be the first time we see who we really are.

The ego is the earth-self in form. It *is* the body and the mind, our energetic walls. It is the structure through which we work, the substance from which we operate here on Earth. We need to know where our limits lie, how we should maintain ourselves and what our image is here. We need an ego.

The true ego that is required to live in the world keeps us engaged, making decisions and enjoying earthly pleasures. All egos are the same.

"When there is purity with the ego,
our true self and the soul can advance.
Our soul knows what it wants.
The ego should follow."

We are meant to have dreams and visions and goals. The road we take to attain them will be revealed day by day. As the road unfolds, we will change. As we change, our ideas and our ideals may change.

In addition to the true ego, however, there is a false ego. A false ego tries to hang on to the fact that the ego can have its *own* identity, that it can be different, and that we can be better than somebody else. It clings to an "I am better than you" vanity. The false ego does not see mankind as it sees itself. The false ego, or false self, is predicated on guilt and maintaining control. It is the false ego that is greedy; the one that feels it is more righteous, or that it can go beyond its own expectations of the human form. This ego becomes mistakenly elevated.

Hosting Darkness

When we feel a need to be different from other people, the difference is not surfacing naturally. Our false egos birth these differences because we think it makes us unique. We are forcing differences because we feel they will serve us, but they are not part of who we truly are. When we give these new false identities power they become their own darkness. We then continue to fortify the identities because they make us feel special. This energy tricks us into confusing specialness with goodness. In this case, special appears to be a good thing even though it is actually negative, and hurts us and others. Darkness, or negativity, feeds through a false ego, and a feeling of grandiose achievement.

"Humility and self-esteem;
the backbone of the spirit.
Humility and self-respect are the building blocks
of the true ego."

True vs. False: Working Through It, the Inner Competition

On Earth, our conscience is part of our higher consciousness. The higher consciousness knows the difference between right and wrong because it is fed from the higher self. The conscience, the higher consciousness and the higher self should all be at work more than our ego. When the ego is not slanted, truth will emerge. The true ego allows what we really want to be present.

When the ego is healed, it becomes a vessel to transport our feelings. Life then becomes available to us. When we are clear, there is no need to worry about why this or why that happens. We just are. We react and move forward.

The true ego allows our inner actions to speak for themselves through a system. This system lets the ego operate the "program of life" smoothly. It runs the show, and it is the show. The ego is our teacher. We literally walk around with our "learning technique." When we feel that we are better than anyone else, to any extent, we sabotage this system and our structure. We dwell on an impossibility – that it is possible to be better than someone else. This can never be accomplished, because it is not true. When we strive to be who we really are in our fullest capacity, the false ego will no longer have our attention. It will dissipate and fall away. It is a game of the self, not a competition. We are meant to excel at anything our being is a part of, and we are allowed to be different. Differences are appreciated and are an exciting part of living. But we are not *better* than one another.

It is paramount to use our feelings wisely when the ego is in a neutral position. We grow within ourselves and we can only grow beyond ourselves. Our own accomplishments can only be succeeded by our own accomplishments. This is the key to life.

"True authority and humility occur simultaneously.
True humility is faith."

Pitfalls of the Ego:

The true ego is supported by real emotions. Real emotions are the different feelings or vibrations that continually reinforce life. Happiness is a real emotion.

False emotions run off their own energy. They have no support. The three major pitfalls that undermine and cripple our true ego are greed, guilt and shame. These are the constraints that help to establish and perpetuate the false ego.

Greed

"Greed: a blinded vision of false capacity."

Greed is a standstill emotion. It is a stifling energy, a reversal of the process of growth. Greed is a self-perpetuating addiction, an emotion that feeds off itself. It cannot be nourished. We are never happy or satisfied. Greed is a sacrifice of life. This false thought immediately shuts down access to our vision and our power.

People can be greedy about many things, both tangible and intangible. Financial wealth is often associated with greed – but the two should not be automatically linked.

Greed & Wealth

Wealth can be looked at in many ways. Vast amounts of money used for our own sake defeats our purpose. We should not be overindulgent, yet we should make every effort to have a happy and prosperous life.

The proper way to look at wealth is with responsibility. Wealth on this planet is not independent from a source of all that is right. Affluence has its place. Whether we have earned wealth, or have acquired it through an act of fate/karma (inherited, through marriage, etc.), we are allowed to be successful. We should know that we can take part in receiving as many gifts as this world has to offer, and that, at the same time, we can replenish the world. Wealth should be used to move forward and lay the groundwork for further accomplishment. It allows us to access pathways to a new world. There is enough wealth in the world for everyone to prosper.

"Our goal is to use wealth
to cultivate ideas and open possibilities
for people, for the Earth, and for ourselves
in a manner of our own calling or choosing."

Gifts

Giving is a gift we are presented with here on Earth. Like wealth, gift-giving, too, has responsibility attached to it.

We should keep in mind what is appropriate and what is not. Gifts should not be given from a feeling of guilt or shame. This never brings relief or fulfillment. Gifts should be given as uncompromised acts of care and affection.

If people use sense and a little intelligence, it can be fun to have money. If it is not fun, something is wrong.

"When comfort, need and satisfaction extinguish greed, the result is prosperity for all."

Guilt

Guilt is a draining issue from the past, a very old way of life, the seemingly endless serpent, the abuser, the perpetrator and the perpetrated. It is a part of the human experience that needs to be alleviated. Guilt is a force. It is one of the greatest wounds of the soul, and we've come here to heal it. When we carry deep-rooted guilt that we may or may not understand, no matter what we do, we feel that we are not capable of attaining happiness.

There are three manifestations of guilt. There is the guilt that actually exists. We are very aware of it because our actions have contributed to creating a wrong. With this type of guilt, we must let our wrong-doing sit, and the process of just being will introduce and join our guilt to shame. They will move along within us until we realize we can genuinely apologize to ourselves, and others involved. If there is karma, a settlement or a retribution to be put into place, it will transpire and the guilt will lift.

There is guilt when realization surfaces after a period of time; when the knowledge that we did something wrong settles in our consciousness. This is guilt as an afterthought. The key, in this case, is to realize and admit that, as human beings, we are fallible. Regardless of the mistakes we may have made or who we were in the past, at that time, we were behaving as a human being. By accepting the aspect of human fault, we become humble. Humility leads to healing.

It is tricky, however. When we think that we are supposed to be perfect and not make any mistakes, we imagine that we ought to be infallible. We deny what it means to be human and it is from *this* point that this form of guilt really originates. We do not necessarily feel guilty for our human error; we feel the guilt from the misbelief that we are supposed to be infallible.

There is also a form of guilt that we are unaware of having. Feelings stir from deep down inside. We feel guilty about *something* and we do not know what it is. This is guilt from the past, or guilt that we may have been led to believe is ours. Whether it is a real guilt or false guilt, as we feel it, it is coming through and being cleansed.

Guilt is a major offender. We may try to get defensive about it. In this case, guilt disguises itself as critical attitude.

A major reason we are on this Earth is to put ourselves in a form where we can be still while we review and proceed with our existence. So even if we feel guilty, regardless of whether something was or was not our fault, by staying with it, feeling it, and living with it, we are forgiving ourselves. We must want to let it go, and then proceed. Our souls can achieve guiltlessness through humility. With all guilt, the lesson to be learned is to stay with it and allow cleansing to occur of its own accord.

There is an answer and that is why we are here.

Shame

"Shame is a frozen point in time –
it is the mending time that brings clarity.
Shame, the unbearable cross, is the identity of guilt."

Shame is a pressure in our hearts that all is not right, but it is an emotion we have the ability to do something about.

Shame needs forgiveness. It follows guilt, and it is the passage that frees us from guilt. If we did not feel shame, there would be no link between guilt and our heart. When we have forgiven ourselves for the guilt, the shame may take its time, but it *will* evaporate once the karma of the guilt is met and forgiveness is felt. Releasing guilt and shame takes a great act of courage, but the relief is well worth the effort.

CHAPTER 5

It is such a blessing that we can feel shame. Shame causes a reversal of fortune. It is able to change our soul's route and release the darkness around us. The word, shame, should be re-defined as "reprieve." It reminds us that we have a second chance to make things right.

CHAPTER 6

Fear
&
Obsession

"Fear – the issue behind all issues."

"Try not to fear the fear of fear."

Fear

Fear : An unpleasant often strong emotion caused by anticipation or awareness of danger.

The definition(s) in italics above are used by permission from Merriam-Webster Online Dictionary ©2004 by Merriam-Webster, Incorporated (www.Merriam-Webster.com).

Everybody is afraid at one time or another. Fear is the energetic barrier that supports all that opposes us. It can hold us down and suppress every natural aspect of our human lives. We are afraid of death, dying, growing old, going insane, getting fat, being too thin, becoming ugly, not being recognized, not succeeding, not having enough money, not being loved, of losing love and of being lost forever. Yet, we are also fearful of success, of being too beautiful, of being recognized, falling in love and of moving forward.

Fear is repetitive and phobic. It can feel like both our strength and our cord with God have been broken. Fear keeps us from really living.

What exactly is fear and why does it hold such power over us? How can we move through it, get rid of it and be free from it?

When we feel afraid of something we need to ask ourselves, "What am I afraid of? What is the purpose of being in this situation?"

Answers always emerge through the opening that fear provides.

CHAPTER 6

"Fear is the backward key to salvation."

Fear is humiliating. It enables a clean break from control. It causes us to let every barrier collapse as truth, strength and power come forward.

Fear is the deterrent of spirit, and its friend. When fear builds, we reach out, we ask for help, we open. Even when we are feeling intense fear, we can still be on a spiritual path. Fear and spirituality do not preclude each other when a healing is taking place. The soul is meant to be with peace.

"Through fear, comes the arrival of hope."

Why we use fear:
Fear is the quickest route to any solution.
There is no such thing as being "too stressed out."
Stress out! Stress out!
Don't be afraid to feel panic.
Panic will not hurt you.
It is just trying to let energy you do not need escape.

Obsession

"Obsession is the banquet for fear.
Fear feeds off obsession."

Obsession : A persistent disturbing preoccupation with an often unreasonable idea or feeling.

The definition(s) in italics above are used by permission from Merriam-Webster Online Dictionary ©2004 by Merriam-Webster, Incorporated (www.Merriam-Webster.com).

Obsession is quiet. An obsessive act is crippling. It is a deep, private inner issue. The mind won't let go. It is a trauma that keeps hitting a wall, over and over again.

The Up-Side of Obsession

Obsession is repetitive and it works on the mind. Obsession may introduce a thought that is so painful to us that it may cause a breakdown/breakthrough when it is not being depressed naturally. If the burden that we are carrying is tremendously arduous, an exaggerated shift becomes necessary. There is no need for concern. The body will alter itself correctly.

When we talk about a trauma, and when we are truly obsessed with that trauma, obsession beats harder.

With obsession, an imbalance, issue and/or fear has surfaced in order to be dispelled. The disturbance(s) may have been buried within us for a very long period of time, and may be deep-rooted. The obsession may carry within it many situations in our lives that need to be altered. When obsession is present, movement is taking place. A negative energy is leaving us as fast as it can, without doing us any real harm.

An obsessive thought is redundant, only because the thought and the discharge of the issue is so powerful that it has to repeat itself in our minds in order for a pattern to be completed.

Obsession is like a basket. It holds any negative action of vibration as it carries a complex issue, and all that it entails, through to a final stage of release.

The pain, burden, dilemma may need to continuously hammer and penetrate so it can eradicate several thought patterns at once. The obsession then encompasses the entire issue.

If we are caught in a fire, the firefighters are persistent about breaking down a door to free us from peril. Over and over again they attack the barrier that stands between our death and our safety. They are obsessive in their cause. Relentless energy trying to save a life is natural obsession. Whether it is an answer we must act on or an answer that is handed to us, obsession is beating down the door of denial to present a breakthrough. As a result, the intense, solid, massive energy that was causing the pain is now dispersed.

The Down-Side of Obsession

There is also an obsession that is not healthy, an *act of obsession*. This is an obsession that takes place to gain attention when we try to control or supervise movement, or when the ego holds on to a situation that it cannot change. When an outcome is determined by our ego, we may think it useful to obsess. We are using *it*, the obsession is not working through us. These are machinations of *false obsession*. "I want that coat. I want that coat." "I want that job." "I want that person to fall in love with me, no matter what."

This is self-inflicted obsession.

"Obsession can be the threshold of relief."

CHAPTER 7

Codependency

"You are not responsible for anyone else.
Caring is enough."

Codependency

Codependent : A psychological condition or a relationship in which a person is controlled or manipulated by another who is affected with a pathological condition (as an addiction to alcohol or heroin).

The definition(s) in italics above are used by permission from Merriam-Webster Online Dictionary ©2004 by Merriam-Webster, Incorporated (www.Merriam-Webster.com).

Codependency is the non-ability to be who you really are. We can be codependent with a person, a job, a situation or a pattern. Worrying about these relationships *is* the codependency. People need only to take care of, and to value, themselves.

Codependency cancels out individuality, and will diminish any kind of self-esteem and self-worth. It is an artificial set-up of what life is about. It is the ability (or rather the *disability*) to dwell on something else other than ourselves and who we are.

"Loneliness is an unsettled emptiness.
When we are truly empty we are open to receive."

Every human being is born alone and dies alone. When we are afraid to be alone with ourselves, it is usually because of codependency. We may not trust our relationship with God and also may not recognize the true value of being with one's own self. At times it is rewarding to settle a negative or disruptive stirring within by choosing solitude. Life wants to prove to us that we can be alone, and that this offers great possibilities.

When we are by ourselves we continuously create pure, new, unobstructed beginnings. Everything essential happens from a naked point. Our unique power is felt when it is not influenced by another. When we are alone, and there is nowhere to turn, there is nothing to distract or hinder a growth process. We have only our own thoughts. This *new* beginning will spark new ideas. This *new self* will ignite another self, which will ignite another, and so forth and so on.

When we are not in a codependent relationship, but with the purity of other people, another type of growth occurs. This growth is different, yet just as essential as the growth we experience when we are alone. This is companionship, not codependency. When two or more minds are working towards a unified mind, the unified mind can work on its own, or it can open possibilities for each individual. This is about love and self-reinforcement. People stimulate each other, and, when we are clear and balanced, the stimulation is pure.

"A relationship does not grow and change;
people grow and change and the relationship follows."

Codependency is a way of not being true to oneself because it seems more satisfying to dwell on others. "Oh, I'll do that for you anytime you want." When deep inside the thought process is; "When and what are you going to do for me?" Or, "I have to worry about him now. I don't have time to think about where I'm headed."

Every life needs structure *and* a free range. With

codependency, we feel a false urgency to achieve something that cannot be accomplished. It keeps us occupied because it involves the act of being in charge. It glamorizes a position of importance. Every aspect of codependency is dangerous and false.

Codependency with a thought pattern turns into false obsession. The codependent obsession is created *by* us – it is not an issue that we are trying to rid ourselves of.

When there is balance created in *any* relationship, codependency cannot exist. What is necessary with relationships is a non-focused looseness of love – just letting it happen. Suffocation and restriction in a relationship is codependency.

In an odd way, codependency is a form of competition. "I'm better than you and I'm going to show you while I pretend to be your friend and take care of you." Or, "I am relying on your kindness for me to feel flattered and exalted."

When we send a message of love to the people we care about, the vibration it carries puts a supportive power around them. If we try to go back and *save* them, we negate this power and are not allowing them to do their own work. The piece of us that wants to save another person is our ego. This is false ego reinforcing false ego. The other person's false ego does not want to do the work. Their true ego does. Only purity can heal. An ego cannot. When we try to save someone, it is an empty act of manipulation, and only holds back all involved.

"No one can be whole with someone else
unless they are whole with themselves.
Love abounds when the presence of oneself is present."

"A person without oneself
is a person without the substance for the start."

Projection

When we project, we are not able to see that we are fallible, so it appears to us that other people have our faults. When we attract people who have similar faults or negative patterns, this may be an indication that we hold these same issues.

Projection itself becomes a form of denial. It keeps us united with codependency.

Also, at times we attract people with the same burdens because it makes us feel comfortable. A person with an addiction will seek out others with the same addiction, because it supports their own addiction. The world looks rosy – we are all addictive. When we surround ourselves with people who have a negative agenda similar to our own, we cannot see the rest of the world. It is a barrier, a self-perpetuating illness. Not only is this projection, this act substantiates an issue.

When we project, we are looking into the mirror. We are showing ourselves *ourselves* through the negativity of another person. We are projecting what scares us inside onto other people.

These other people will stay in our life until we realize, "That is me I'm seeing. I don't want this anymore. I see that I am projecting and that this is *my* issue. I don't need to attract people with that issue. I need relief for myself. I can let this situation go now."

By focusing on the fact that something in us is broken, or not functioning correctly, half the battle is already won. Recognition will provide a pathway for the remainder of the release to become active. Through projection we become aware of our own shortcomings through another person. We are experiencing reflection. At times this is also karma because we are bringing other people in to point out our misguided ways; we are mirroring each other.

When our relationships are healthy, the entrances and closures of life occur with graciousness. We can create and then exit. Our life phases will culminate with respect and satisfaction. We cannot ask for anything more when we leave this Earth than to have achieved proper endings.

CHAPTER 8

Anger
Compulsion & Addiction
Jealousy

"Anger precedes fear.
But fear, at times, turns into anger.
Once the fear is recognized and confronted,
it will release and leave
through a natural act of anger.
Active discharge of anger is a discharge of fear."

Anger

"Abuse: the frozen tyrant."

Anger : A strong feeling of displeasure and usually of antagonism. Rage. Synonyms anger, ire, rage, fury, indignation, wrath mean an intense emotional state induced by displeasure.

The definition(s) in italics above are used by permission from Merriam-Webster Online Dictionary ©2004 by Merriam-Webster, Incorporated (www.Merriam-Webster.com).

Anger is the plug that separates the human being from passion.

Anger is stunted passion. It is an overt feeling or emotion and needs to be displayed. Anger is meant to be expressed naturally; which can be tricky, delicate and very difficult to do.

There is a great deal of anger in the world today for various reasons. There are a lot of people trying to get along with a lot of other people. There are many different belief systems and many, many false prejudices.

How Did I Get All This Anger?

When we are in pain, we get angry. When we are held back from the glory of life's possibilities and/or the continuous feeling of pleasure and joy, we get angry. When someone we love is hurt, we get angry. When we are sad, fearful and despondent, we get angry. When we are abused, we get angry.

When anger is denied and is stored up, bottled up or put on hold for too long, it is probable that we will enter into a defensive state; a false self-protective state. The anger seeps into itself and then breaks apart; causing irrational rage, bitterness and vindictive behavior. We become unapproachable, and we are resentful toward others. This dangerous buildup can also cause us to become slanted and warped.

Anger can be healthy. The reason we are angry is that the energetic power from our soul (our identity) has been limited, or shut down, by a series of incidences or by someone. We may believe that some situation, some person, or even God, is not seeing us for what we truly are. We are left out, misinterpreted, abandoned. We get angry when we hurt. It is painful to be angry. Healthy anger is presented into our lives when we need to stand up for ourselves, when we do not feel something is fair, or when we need to take steps forward.

"When self-worth is realized and felt,
anger will disperse."

Natural Anger – Feeling It and Dispersing It

Anger creates an accumulation of energy that needs to be released one way or another. This initiates both a formula and a vehicle for the release of the stored-up blockages of energy that are caused by doubt and suffering. When we realize that we are angry, we create a balance between the anger and recognition.

Anger is the water that comes through the faucet once the handle is turned. It lies deep within us whenever there is friction. When we are angry, at times we feel it is inappropriate to respond immediately. But anger is our most active primal emotion; and when we feel it, we need to display it naturally.

Anger is expressed through rapid discharges of emotion. We can be creative with it; we can exercise through it, cry through it, and we can try to voice it, but it has to be recognized and acknowledged in some way. If we are truly hurt and/or compromised, anger is appropriate.

Confrontation is our best offense with present or everyday feelings of anger, and it is the best partner for cleansing these feelings. It is best to respond correctly and efficiently. If reasonable anger is not transmuted immediately, eventually the anger will push itself down and collect deep within. The feelings incurred through neglect and attack do not just disappear naturally. Somewhere along the line we must stand up for ourselves and face these angry feelings. We must react.

On a physical level, exercise can be advantageous in healing anger. Through this, we become more aware of the value of physical movement. Inadvertently, the connection between the body and the mind becomes more apparent through the release of anger.

On the emotional level, we must make an inner choice to heal. Contact with other people to further assess what is happening in our own lives can be beneficial. When we reach out we bring comfort to ourselves. Comfort and understanding from another soul is invaluable and essential.

"True human compassion delivers."

Another component to healing anger involves working with ourselves from within. The higher self will provide an outlet in our daily life routine. We may find at times, that incidences trigger off *erratic responses*. We may react harshly to something we did not even realize irritated us. This is anger playing itself out. A stage is set which provides us with a way to release the anger, and we work towards a solution. The energy from the anger that was held in is now dispelled, which will benefit all circumstances and relationships involved with the buildup of that particular anger.

Compulsion & Addiction

Compulsion : An act of compelling : the state of being compelled. A force that compels. An irresistible impulse to perform an irrational act.

Addiction : The quality or state of being addicted. Compulsive need for and use of a habit-forming substance (as heroin, nicotine, or alcohol) characterized by tolerance and by well-defined physiological symptoms upon withdrawal; broadly : persistent compulsive use of a substance known by the user to be harmful .

The definition(s) in italics above are used by permission from Merriam-Webster Online Dictionary ©2004 by Merriam-Webster, Incorporated (www.Merriam-Webster.com).

Compulsion and addiction are forms of anger. Both use external behavior to create a scene. They are born from a pattern of *searching so desperately* to try to fill the emptiness inside of oneself. Both compulsive and addictive acts are cries for help. "I'm hurting."

When we want to release the dam of anger from inside, and we do not recognize that what we are feeling is anger, addictive and compulsive behavior may take over. In reality, we are wrestling within ourselves to get rid of an irritant. The false ego does not let us focus on the distress. Our emotions will connect to the routine of living and cause us to become compulsive and/or addictive because they have nowhere to be known or seen.

Compulsive and addictive people are twisting a forceful element of fire (which is meant to be passion) to suit an unreal, imaginative or artificial need. The behavior might express itself as smoking, eating, drinking alcohol, gambling, using drugs, shopping, sex, etc. Regardless of how it manifests itself, it is born from a restlessness within.

Anger is not an easy emotion to live with, but we have to match the reaction of anger with another reaction. We do not need to control the action. Compulsion and addiction are controlled actions; true reaction is not.

Compulsion tries to hurt. It is an overt action, a display. Compulsion takes hold when there is so much rage and frustrated energy inside that the energy needs to be channeled elsewhere. An answer cannot be found, so we focus our efforts on making a desired answer happen. We then lash out instead of seeing that the turmoil lies deep within us. In this case, we almost seek revenge for our anger. There would not be compulsive behavior if we realized that the anger was our own and that it was acceptable to feel it.

Compulsion is a rapid display of anger, whereas addiction is a slower, self-inflicted form of anger. When any uncontrollable phase comes into our lives, it has great purpose.

"Compulsion acts before there is fear.
Addiction waits for fear and then reacts."

With addiction, we are trying to hurt ourselves. Addiction occurs when something inside of us hurts tremendously. The pain shakes us deeply within; and, in our reluctance or denial to accept that there can be a real answer, we push the pain down. We create addictions. It is unresolved faith. We are so afraid to face the pain and let it come through that we go into a pattern. When we feel the pain, we block it. Over and over again, this blockage creates an addiction, a repetitive force of anger that is confined, but because it is anger, it will seep out eventually. Subconsciously with addiction, sooner or later, we create a scene. It is a cry for help. Addiction: all or nothing.

When we show compassion for ourselves and we begin to acknowledge an addiction or a control issue or a compulsive behavior, the battle is half-won. The right combination is there. "I am human, I am not perfect and I am hurting."

When we feel that we have been betrayed, or left out, or that life has not worked out for us so far, we may carry an attitude. "What about me? Why am I forgotten?" We are never forgotten. We are learning and are being challenged to look at an issue, or to carry out a mission or to face karma. During this period we are completing a major part of our healing life. We are trying to reach a proper ending to an important period of our life and then we will move on.

Control Using Commitment

Everyone wants to tell a story. We all want to impart our own tale. Sometimes, we commit to the story before it unfolds. This makes us feel special. We feel complete when a situation in our life has a beginning, a middle and an end. We may decide to create any part of this while it is still transpiring. We wear a *story,* this commitment, like a badge. This is also codependent because we want to belong, we want to be in charge. "I've made it. I've succeeded. My story is complete. I can tell everyone. I can feel good about myself. Look what I've accomplished."

When we sense an urgency to finish what we set out to do, or we become confused and feel left out because the answer to our life has not surfaced yet, we push for (and may even make up) a conclusion.

"It's time for me to get married. I'll get married now. Everything will be all right. I'll just marry this person because I am with him or her now."

"I want my business to move forward. It should have by now. I'll take on some larger clients, or some more clients, even if I am not ready and they are not the people I want to be associated with in the long run. Financially, this will be a positive move. I need to expand now."

"It's time for me to have a baby and buy a house. Everybody has them. I think this would be good for me. I don't know where I'll get the money for a house, or if I have the patience for a child. But there will be help if I need it. It will be okay. I am moving forward now."

This story-telling is about codependency, addiction and compulsion. We predestine our destination. We are trying to control larger situations in our lives, when in reality, they have their own natural sequence.

When addiction is blended with the element of succeeding and finishing a story, *more* is appealing. More eating, more smoking, more drinking. "If I have more it will feel better." "Well, I've spent $20 on a bet, why not the whole $100? I may win! If not, there is only $80 left in my pocket. So what? I'll start again tomorrow."

Overindulgent behavior and procrastination never provide accomplishment.

"Anger is attached to jealousy.
Jealousy is anger's little brother."

Jealousy

*Jealous : Intolerant of rivalry or unfaithfulness. Disposed
to suspect rivalry or unfaithfulness. Hostile toward a rival or
one believed to enjoy an advantage.*

The definition(s) in italics above are used by permission from Merriam-Webster Online Dictionary
©2004 by Merriam-Webster, Incorporated (www.Merriam-Webster.com).

Jealousy is an uncomplicated emotion that causes much hidden pain and perplexity.

Jealousy is the inability to feel safe and secure with our connection to what truth is and that which lies beyond what is visible to us now.

Jealousy, at its best, is the realization that we are caught in our own restless need to have something or someone.

"Why am I jealous? I try so hard not to be jealous."

We do not understand it, but we accept that we are feeling it. It is obvious to us, and we are ashamed.

On the other hand, where there is a ruthless attack aimed at another person because of one's possessive thoughts, the result is rage, pain and fear. This is jealousy at its worst.

Jealousy stems from the inability to know oneself, to thrive with oneself, and to be proud of oneself.

Jealousy insists on capturing a person or what they have, and owning *it*. "Be mine. I can't be mine." We thrash out at our target in anger because this can never be accomplished.

The solution to jealousy lies in evaluating ourselves and our own moral standards. When we have self-respect, we allow morality to come into our life.

If jealous rage bites heavily at our hearts, and it feels irrational (or if it becomes a repetitive thought) we need to first apologize to ourselves for feeling broken and intensely domineering over someone else. Then we should speak to the other person about our irrational feelings. Allow them to help. They may be able to give us the space to re-evaluate, to ease the guilt, and to reassure us that the jealousy is unfounded.

Once jealousy is recognized, shame can be felt. Tears may follow. Cleansing will take place.

If feelings of neglect are founded, which may occur with someone we hold close, we need a comforting answer. We all have special connections with the different people in our lives. That is what makes each relationship unique. We need support and caring. If this need is not met, there is sadness and pain. When the relationship does not foster individual growth and love, we should let go and move away from the situation.

CHAPTER 9

Depression

*"Depression is the passive force
behind a breakthrough."*

Depression

Depression : An act of depressing or a state of being depressed. A state of feeling sad : dejection. A psychoneurotic or psychotic disorder marked especially by sadness, inactivity, difficulty in thinking and concentration, a significant increase or decrease in appetite and time spent sleeping, feelings of dejection and hopelessness, and sometimes suicidal tendencies. A reduction in activity, amount, quality, or force. A lowering of vitality or functional activity.

The definition(s) in italics above are used by permission from Merriam-Webster Online Dictionary ©2004 by Merriam-Webster, Incorporated (www.Merriam-Webster.com).

Depression is valuable and healthy, and is often necessary for healing. There are two types of depression, true and false. The symptoms of both types appear to be the same, but the depressions are not the same. Depression is a natural *slowing down* of our human system and it can cause panic if it is not understood properly.

True Depression

Depression is a non-active state of being. It is necessary to sit still with it. We usually do not feel comfortable when we need to be inactive. When we seek an answer over and over again, and nothing surfaces, the body may sink into a true depression. When our intent is to move forward, but the mind gets cloudy, the body depresses. So when we are stagnant, because the mind has too much to think about, we may partially shut down. This may appear as a type of laziness, but it is a depression of the mind setting in. This is a natural function of our system; therefore, it is to be expected.

Depression is also an active state because it provides a means to an end. The understanding of an issue becomes more available to us. We depress the negative way we react to our perception of issues, energetic feelings and solutions. It is necessary for us to allow the comprehension of these feelings to come through in segments, so we are not overwhelmed. Depression is a self-protection mechanism. Experiencing intervals of depression is one of the natural rhythms of the human being. The action of depression holds back an energetic field while the field comes through. We may still be evolving and changing, but we have merely shut off a thought process because it is too much to think about.

True depression is the irony of healing. It really works. It is an awkward state because it mimics a refusal to see something, when in actuality we may be seeing so clearly that we are seeing too much at once. When called for, true depression will make itself available to assist fear, obsession, anger, addiction and compulsion. True depression works with us and serves the purpose of creating pauses as we move forward.

At times, we should ask for support through true depression to help us eliminate the fear that may be caused by a dormant state of being. Also, movement in the other areas of our life that we *can* control is important and helpful. Participating in any sport or exercise, walking, enjoying entertainment, being in nature and especially around water, or conversation about the lighter aspects of life, whenever possible, can be beneficial.

False Depression

False depression hangs on purposeful denial. We may hold on to a pattern, or a negative emotion, that needs to be released. We feel this serves us. We create a state of inertia because we cannot get what we want. "I am depressed. I do not want to move forward." This depression is about using stagnation to get attention, instead of growing and moving ahead. If we are depressed, other people will think that we are in pain. They will leave us alone with our own pity, and we will be allowed to keep this false state of hopelessness. When we use depression in this way, we do not have to look at our own issues because we have manipulated a holding ground for them. The false depression becomes a way of life.

A Twist With False Depression

"Coulda... woulda... shoulda..." is a depression that focuses on the past because we do not realize a truth; that we can start our lives anew from wherever we are. We want to change the outcome of a situation that has transpired. And that cannot possibly occur.

Instead, we must use the present to create new openings which will provide new solutions. We are always at the beginning. When we dwell on what has been, we infect ourselves with bitterness. There is no reason to be depressed over the past. The past will catch up with the future once we let go of the idea that we cannot control it.

CHAPTER 9

"When someone is seemingly moving forward,
they may be standing still.
Conversely, when we are standing still –
we may be moving forward."

CHAPTER 10

Breakdown/Breakthrough

"Cleared human passion reveals beginnings."

Breakdown/Breakthrough

"I'm doing everything right,
why is everything going wrong?"

Breakdown : The action or result of breaking down: as a fail-
ure to function, a failure to progress or have effect. A physi-
cal, mental, or nervous collapse. The process of
decomposing.

Breakthrough : An act or instance of breaking through an
obstruction. A sudden advance especially in knowledge or
technique (a medical breakthrough). A person's first
notable success.

The definition(s) in italics above are used by permission from Merriam-Webster Online Dictionary
©2004 by Merriam-Webster, Incorporated (www.Merriam-Webster.com).

Breakdown

"When things seem to go backwards."

When we are involved with a breakdown, no matter how it is termed, release is felt with a backward motion. The negativity and/or build-up of unnecessary energy is of such magnitude that panic, insanity or trauma may be required to find release.

Breakdown is *emotion going backwards* very quickly to eradicate negative build-up and patterning within us. This leaves a perfect opening for new life to begin. A breakdown is like the wave that comes upon the shore. It rushes forward on the sand and, as the wave retreats with its backward motion, it cleanses anything that stands in the way. This motion is very valuable. It is not negative. It is active, not passive. This backwards motion in healing always results in a cleanse.

A *breakdown/breakthrough* creates the groundwork for us to let go of what we thought was our completed system. Now we are ready to change. The body may seem like it is breaking apart, and the spine and the nervous system are giving way. We may feel that what we are experiencing is wrong, crazy, or insane, but what is happening should be congratulated. It is not a deformed, twisted complication.

A breakdown does not happen in order to bring a matter to our attention. It is, rather, a movement of forceful energy to let go of old patterning, or it is a forceful entry to introduce new life. Both of these things may happen simultaneously, or they can happen separately – but they happen within some sequence of time that is relevant to each other. When we are psychically and emotionally ready to advance to another level, or to let go of a huge pattern or situation, or even a relationship that is no longer necessary, there could be a breakdown.

When an illness strikes, the body goes through a physical breakdown. In this case, a breakdown or a trauma in one's life is an accented point of energy that is allowing something to free-up.

A *breakdown* is always connected to a *breakthrough*.

"The extreme force of loss is a state of adjustment."

Panic

Panic may take place when a breakdown is trying to happen. If the nervous system is on edge or getting ready to change rapidly, panic may set in. The nervous system is the controller of peace and fear.

Panic is a raw, unidentifiable current of energy. It occurs when our breathing literally gets stuck and cannot circulate through our body's system. We do not get enough oxygen. It is as if we are collapsing and the energy is too much to hold. Panic is an alteration of air and life.

When we sense we are losing control, or when something is an intense burden on our minds, we often panic. In this panic, the nervous system is *positioned out of its own self,* so air and life get confused, and they hit against each other. We need to let go – there is an extreme exit. We panic. This is part of a formula.

Society has not taught us how to fall apart, give way and give in properly. The body is operating in a way that acknowledges a breakthrough. Let the mind hold onto whatever it needs in order to get through this period of acute vulnerability (trust, logic, even the panic itself), or just feel totally out of control. An answer will be given because the body knows that when we are breaking down, we are breaking through.

Both trauma and insanity are part of a breakdown/ breakthrough.

Trauma

Trauma is the universal feeling of friction. It can be felt in many situations (not only in breakdown/breakthrough) and for many reasons. A trauma in our life is an accented point of energy that allows our life force to expand. A sudden acceleration in the human psyche may cause trauma.

Trauma is most often looked at through the eyes of fear. If we were to take those eyes, and replace them with the eyes of trust, the road and the process through trauma and breakdown/breakthrough would happen less painfully and, probably, more swiftly.

A trauma may break up an old paradigm, or set up a new one, without any anticipation or warning. Human nature is working directly with us. We have called on a situation with great intent to bring new life into its beginning. Now that the trauma has exposed our new life, healing can take place. Trauma may also be a course taken to rid us of old negative karma.

Insanity

Insanity is its own void. Intense, scattered energy lies within the personality of insanity. The effect is that the human being becomes disjointed, or too raw, to make sense. This period of insanity is filled with a mixture of anger and rage. The purpose of insanity is to experience a heavy discharge before proceeding to the next level of development and human purpose. The void of insanity works within the void of genius as insanity runs its course.

Insanity is *change happening backwards*. The energy releases in reverse in order to clear the ego of extreme negative patterning. This release happens purposefully, beyond our control.

When we are *insane* we are acting out, even if there is no awareness. The observer to insanity becomes fearful because the episodic craziness seems and feels foreign or absurd. In reality, this is reminding the observer of some deep association to the past that went amiss; a real memory, or an experience that *they* have been through.

Insanity is what takes place when a breakthrough is put on hold for a while because the ego has had trouble letting go. Insanity is the erratic action of the true being severing itself apart in order to stay open so that it can release distorted energy. As we feel more secure with ourselves and as the ego lets go, nature can then take charge.

"Insanity: the place where the soul re-introduces itself."

"Insanity is the pause between what is right and what has been wrong. It might be a form of karma that is meant to turn around."

Insanity causes great controversy and it requires its own timing. Insanity may look to the outsider like a horrific, fearful imbalance, and appears to be the harshest form of rearrangement for the being. The struggle appears to be so difficult, and inexplicable, but a miraculous situation is being held in place so that the ego can let go. There is always protection with this process. Because of the open space that is created, a new force will surge through, creating a new person. Karma surfaces, and a period of immense karmic change takes place.

"Anger is met with patience in the most exposed manner
– insanity."

Multiple personalities and schizophrenic behaviors, like insanity, are altered states. But within schizophrenia or multiple personalities, the person will divert their true energy because they have been so damaged in a primal area of their being. Once they feel safe enough to come back together, they will. If the insane person, the schizophrenic or the person with multiple personalities feels enough trust and acceptance through love, all walls will break down.

If the insane were allowed to rage, in an authentic manner, and acting-out was eliminated, they would fall apart and then re-collect and rebuild. Once a wound is unwound, there is nothing left; and so begins a new way.

It cannot be stressed enough how emotionally upsetting and off-balancing these phases of life can be. At their worst they are relentless and debilitating. All this may seem unfair. But at the deepest point of our existence, there is reason and there is relief.

A breakdown/breakthrough can be simple or it can be more expansive.

Breakthrough

Breakthrough is the advantage of a breakdown.
Anytime a breakdown takes place,
a breakthrough is available.
A void is created here – the void of goodness,
of letting go.

"A breakthrough is a brilliant measure of time received."

We may feel drained and empty after a breakdown.
Rest is called for after a breakthrough.
A breakthrough allows:
new perspective of body, mind and soul,
new ways of acting within oneself and towards others,
new entrances to life.

A breakdown/breakthrough *always* leads to new life.

CHAPTER 11

Balance

"Balance catches us.
It protects us from being absurd and lets us travel to each
corner of existence."

"Balance; the endless imagination."

Balance

Balance : A means of judging or deciding. A counterbalancing weight, force or influence. An aesthetically pleasing integration of elements. A physical equilibrium. The ability to retain one's balance. Mental and emotional steadiness.

The definition(s) in italics above are used by permission from Merriam-Webster Online Dictionary ©2004 by Merriam-Webster, Incorporated (www.Merriam-Webster.com).

Balance is the operating point
from where all energy functions.
Life is balance.
Life is monumental; the power is moving at all times,
even through stillness.
There is always a morning after.
We step out into a new existence.

Balance is natural. It is the place from where genuine peace is known. It is not static. Balance protects us from being ruled by unhealthy extremes. These extremes may cause us to break apart and fracture. They challenge us and produce new problems. We then, need to go back and learn once more.

"Sensation can happen in a moment,
if conditions are correct."

Our spirit works in a way that is accessible to us at any moment. This process is a give and take. Our spirit knows when we are ready to proceed further. We give in – it comes through. When we stay in balance we can override the basic structures of life. Balance gives rise to limitless expansion. Balance is not boring.

The system on Earth is a dance of vibration and balance. Every human being is placed in this world to do their "chore work," and then to move forward and succeed with their dreams. If the world were truly balanced, this would be possible.

Earth

As individuals, each of us needs to focus on ourselves. Nature is protected. It will always take itself back to balance. It knows how and so do we.

Since we are in a *system* here on Earth, the episodes of our lives unfold through a sequence. They have a beginning, an end; and, therefore, must also have an in-between. A system, by the very nature of what it is, upholds and gravitates towards balance. It needs balance. As we evolve, balance will become an established, respected condition; and we will break out of this sequential system. Once we show enough respect to the course of life, balance becomes systematic. Balance is like carving out and walking the path of a circle. Once the path has been established, we do not need to continue to dig in any further. We still have our original circle, but we are now free to expand upon it, thus making our circle larger and wider, as we effortlessly walk the path of balance that we have previously set before us.

"Comfort is the position of a forward motion."

How Balance is Achieved

Balance is produced when we let go of the detailed expectations that we do not have control over. We create a new slate, a blank surface, and an environment for change.

By maintaining equilibrium with our bodies through a healthy regimen of diet, exercise and rest, we are establishing what is necessary to bring balance through the human form. Eventually, or when we are clear, this systematic way of working with both the body/mind and psyche, will become a matter of course. We will not have to ponder about what is in balance and what is not. Guidance is internal and eternal.

We are meant to experience much more than balance, and we will. Balance is the point of humility where all the excitement begins. If we are aware of our inner feelings and we are clear, we are always in balance.

"Perspective is in the eye of the beholder.
Perception is the eye of the mind."

Competition

When there is an ego-based competitive twist to our lives, a desire to put oneself above others (whether with family, friends, in matters of business, or even between nations), balance is removed. When we divide the power of humanity outside of ourselves, we deplete our own power. However, when we strive for excellence with ourselves (to produce, go further, to feel more fulfilled) we are creating balance. There is no competition. We are returning to coexistence and a co-creative experience.

"Equality is a reverence with God."

Evolution & Equality

All human beings endure various degrees and types of fear, and suffer difficult or disastrous situations. If we compare our individual lives to those of other people, the results often appear to be incredibly unjust. There are manifestations of growth and power that present themselves at every moment. There are various *evolutions* here on this Earth. In other words, there are differences in the stages and levels of evolutionary growth. It is all distributed masterfully, but it may not always be apparent or make sense to us. It is moral, it is equal, but it is not the same.

There is a balance of creation going on that exceeds the usual appearance of what is fair. If we attempt to judge this, we shortchange who we are by definition. As evolution continues and is ever present, the rewards, growth, stability, the success of the soul and the happiness within are as unquestionable as they are monumental to what is achieved through devastating growth. All experiences are unique, and balance, at *all* times, is activated when natural episodes progress.

    The evolution of the Earth, the souls that are here and equality are all natural parts of balance. It may seem almost impossible that the three could be synchronous, but through a higher natural movement they are. This is the miracle of balance that we do not understand.

PREAMBLE TO CHAPTER 12

"Almighty power is not diluted even through simplicity, for divine presence is universal, objective and subjective."

There is a divinity, an ever-present acceptance of peace and love – a form and, yet, not.

Our beliefs thrive far beyond this world and this existence. We may not feel it all the time, we may not even believe it is there, but, somehow, it abides. If a deity or a collective of deities did not exist, then why is the force of that existence so prominent to our subconscious? Or to the primal connections of our past? Or to our fight or flight relationship with our deep inner-self? When these connections are made, intelligence is being used with energetic patterns, and *it* becomes a higher scheme of matter.

Higher forms of feeling such as compassion, stability and acts of forgiveness would not exist, or could not be felt, if a higher power did not prevail. How would we cry, rage, love, hate or even go into depression if there were not more? How would we think? Where does it come from? All of these thoughts and feelings would not exist. Science cannot cover it all, for faith, truth and spiritual comprehension exceed any world of science.

Time and time again we question: does something else exist? Is there divine power? Is there divine hope?

We ask these questions because this space, this Earth, has only been able to show us a small, capsulated indication of order, miracles, strength and insightful knowledge. Maybe we have not yet evolved to where we could properly take advantage of these expansive capabilities. So, perhaps this is why for many they do not yet exist.

In this book, and in this chapter, we call this higher power and these concepts "God." We could call God by many names for many purposes of belief.

This book does not presume to judge *any* religious belief or spiritual higher way of thought, or acknowledgement of a higher being. We are all equal, and any belief – when practiced through goodness, cooperation and equality – is valid.

"Hell is an obsessive repetitive space in time."

The thoughts and fears of a demonic presence have been in existence for as long as man's mind has been in existence. They stand between man and God. There are many names and symbols associated with this entity. The fear that surrounds this devil-like being, has been, *and still is,* so great that it may even be held in a type of curious awe. When we sensationalize the devil, or put it on a higher plane, we *create* a holding ground for *it*.

There is also a great deal of superstition and taboo attached to this subject. These erroneous beliefs, or cult-like fears, have escalated at different periods of time and throughout different parts of the world, reinforcing this dark pattern, this unbeatable entity, or this power.

This darkness has been referred to as Lucifer, the devil, Satan, etc. We will call this presence "the devil," but we consider it a defeatable evil.

CHAPTER 12

The Devil
The Voids
Death
God

"Divinity emerges; all makes sense."

"Everlasting truth and energy are always in motion. Truth is more than energy, but spiritual energy is part of truth. Truth is God."

"If all the world loved the way it should, we would all be just fine."

Some of the information in this chapter may have been put forth in earlier portions of this book; however, it is important to re-introduce certain concepts within the context of this material.

The Devil

Devil : 1 often capitalized : the personal supreme spirit of evil often represented in Jewish and Christian belief as the tempter of mankind, the leader of all apostate angels, and the ruler of hell -- usually used with the; often used as an interjection, an intensive, or a generalized term of abuse (what the devil is this?) (the devil you say!)   Christian Science: the opposite of Truth: a belief in sin, sickness, and death: evil, error.

The definition(s) in italics above are used by permission from Merriam-Webster Online Dictionary ©2004 by Merriam-Webster, Incorporated (www.Merriam-Webster.com).

"There is evil. It has been created. It has a power of its own and must be stopped."

The devil is an evil quest happening.
The evil quest keeps it enticed.
The devil has no time, but it interrupts time.
It has no home. The devil *roams* looking for homes.
Hell is the being of the devil.
The devil is any dark egotistical imbalance.

When enough thoughts of negativity are brought together, an evil grows and festers. It takes on an identity of its own. It becomes a force. Sometimes this force cannot literally be seen, so we think of it as a supernatural being. It becomes *something* we are afraid of, *something* that we had nothing to do with, *something* that is not part of this Earth. The devil is very much a part of this Earth.

The devil comes in many forms, each manifests

through an element of fear. The devil tries to use fear as its instrument of "breakage" into the spirit. Fear is accessible because it is an open, sterile platform of suggestion. When we ignore our own ability to create change, we give this force energy. We can change situations and the course of our lives. When we transmute the fear within us, we work with ourselves to dismantle the devil, and the devil will dismantle itself.

Any negative action of energy needs to be reinforced through a projection of itself, or it will die. As evil lives, it takes on a coat of human frailty: ego, delusion, harshness, abuse, violence. This allows evil to feel fulfilled with a strange false power. Each one of these pitfalls looks for more of its own kind, in its own image, so it can breed and perpetuate. For example, codependency needs codependency, addiction needs addiction, false obsession needs more obsessive thought patterns around it to survive.

Our false ego is part of the reason the devil has existed for this long. It is ever-present now because it is being fed. When we heal, the devil will be extinguished. The devil will have no place to dwell, and it will retreat.

Purity does not need energy to survive. Purity resonates through its own power – because it just *is*.

Incognito

There is another aspect to what *seems* devilish in our lives. When an issue is ready to be healed, or we are moving forward with a mission, or if we are settling karma, the healing that is involved may materialize as an uncomfortable or horrific act, which can all be hellish. We may feel misguided, as if we are on the wrong track. When the issue, mission, or karma displays severe consequences, the pain is brought to our attention and we cannot ignore it. This is purity at play as a trickster. This trickster, the *devil incognito*, is a blessing in disguise.

When we are faced with an issue, the devil incognito presents itself as a devilish occurrence in our lives. The energy involved in getting our attention can seem unfair and horrendous, but it must be severe in order to *match* or *mirror* the intensity of the rooted issue. When it is our own issue, the trickster will trip us up within our own body. It allows us to feel we are out of control, and through this loss of control we give up and release what we have been holding on to.

The trickster will also aid us in healing a mission we have chosen to take on. In this case, a purity becomes the devil incognito by disguising itself as an issue. We give up a part of ourselves to heal another area of life, the world, or a core issue of fellow human beings. In this case, the situations, or the people that are being healed, are led through us to an area of understanding and healing that they have not experienced before.

How does this happen?

The pure energy of the trickster will go into our being and simulate the pain, the struggle and the darkness of what we, as healers, intend to ultimately override and conquer. Like an antidote, the pure energy mimics, entices and envelops the severity of the devilish pain and false power. It plunges into the chaotic depths within us, within the being, or within the situation. It captures the true issue, act, pattern or circumstance that has caused grief and setback and pulls them out by the roots. Anyone can be a healer. Anyone can have a mission. When a mission has been healed, we as healers, release the positive aspects of the mission, wherein the answer is found.

When there is karma to work through, we present our own trickster to ourselves because we want to release the shame we feel from past deeds or incidences that we were involved in and with. We want to again feel the pain or discomfort and confusion that we have caused, or silently witnessed without actively trying to reconcile them. We do this so we can be sure that we will not repeat our knowingly misguided ignorance, hurtful acts, injustice, apathy or egotistical naivety. We want to be held accountable for our past actions. We want to change and bring about change. We want to start over.

"Negative karma is the lapse of time
in the wrong direction, and that is hell."

Self-realization and self-worth are the roots of strong

decision-making. They are gifts that this earth can bestow upon us. Our ability as human beings to make the right choices and decisions is so valuable that our higher selves would rather see our bodies and emotions be devastated and/or severely altered, in order for our spirits to triumph and be free. The spirit will not compromise. The soul will always win.

Regardless of the reason the devil incognito appears (issue, mission, or karma), in the end we are left with purity and the strength of our being. We are left with passion, freedom and peace.

The Complex Devil

Aside from our issues, the devil is also a force that is outside of this Earth. This is the "devil" that is a bit closer to what has been traditionally portrayed. There exists an accumulation of negative thought patterns, energy and soul energy that has gone awry, run amok. Bits and pieces of souls have broken off from themselves and have become devilish, dark and foreboding. These cluster-like entities of devilish intent, survive through the false power of themselves. The devil is a structure of incoherent soul energy. It is a system that has gathered up the pretense of itself. Within its truest potency, this force can be destroyed. The devil can be conquered.

"No matter how deep the core of a person journeys into darkness, light can always travel past that, pick it up and change the route."

There is a God
and there is a false essence called the devil
that holds a god-like seduction within it.
The devil is an extraction from the forces of goodness
that have turned against themselves
and have turned against that which is.
The devil's false power, its core existence,
is only involved with itself.
Its presence spins chaotically through its unnatural control.

We are universal and of the life within that universe. The natural forces that preside within ourselves need to be healed in order to surface and direct us. Once our own sense of value is made strong, and we discover who we truly are, we automatically take away a part of what this devil-essence is made of. The devil will have nowhere to turn. Bit by bit it will extinguish.

Higher "battles"
(which in its truth means confrontations),
are exposed and challenged in ways we cannot comprehend.
The simplicity of earthly joy, when felt, lends itself
to a breath, and this breath alters the devil's breath.
Without breath, the devil changes and asks for help
and transformation through a mighty humbleness.
We should feel safe in the knowledge
that there is a realm of purity far past this one,
and yet, so close that it does exist.
Beyond the meaning of the devil,
and far, far beyond its existence,
lies greatness and profound peace.

All we need to be concerned with
is to bring healing to ourselves,
and *then* to this world.

The Voids

*Void : Opening, gap. Empty space: emptiness, vacuum.
The quality or state of being without something: lack, ab-
sence. A feeling of want or hollowness.*

The definition(s) in italics above are used by permission from Merriam-Webster Online
Dictionary ©2004 by Merriam-Webster, Incorporated (www.Merriam-Webster.com).

"The void is a pure space we do not know about."

When we get to a point where we are in between two
situations and the mind opens to an empty space, or we are
afraid to be alone, or we feel like we are breaking down, we
are in a "void."

A void is the pause, the calculated breath, the vacant
period or gap in time that we experience on the physical,
emotional, or soul-felt level. It is the *empty input*. The void
is a great teacher and a miracle-worker. It is the carrier of
change.

Here on earth we encounter and experience feelings
of being stuck in darkness. As human beings, we are terri-
fied to be in a void. We feel imprisoned and held hostage by
it. Yet, no one should be afraid of a void, of this emptiness.
Emptiness is a space that is not tainted by any influence. We
are often frightened of the uncertainty of what the end result
will be, but the void always knows where it is taking us.

The experiences and engagements of our lives will bring up different types of voids. This space and the way we comprehend it may be minor or severe; but it is the holding ground for circumstances that need to be drawn out, or encapsulated, or put into a fast-moving form.

Regardless of how it is presented to us, the key to working with this vehicle of change is to surrender our desire for control and our need to know where we will land. When we surrender to these pauses here on Earth, we create an opportunity to move forward with them. By doing this we prove that we are able to use these spaces in time at our own discretion. Our higher power will allow us to think within the void. We will get to a point where we will actually begin to create our own voids in order to *spread time apart* – to learn, to advance or achieve our goals. The voids are not using and recreating us. We are recreating us.

The void always creates passageways to more evolved and beneficial ways of living.

The Dark Void

The dark void is a false void. It is the void of fear; the fear of the unknown, the fear of relinquishing control. It is the inability to make sense of anything. We fall deeper into the emptiness of the unknown – dark, annihilating and suffocating. This void appears as a dangerous pause, rather than an open connection. It may seem we are cascading downward without hope.

Light will still emerge. We will still emerge.

We are able to use the void as a guideline when fear and panic are involved with it. Through the pain, we cause another realm to open up to us, and through that realm we will see light – we will see God. This may occur because of an outside situation (a house on fire, a death), an internal trauma (questioning oneself over and over again), or a breakdown. An answer is being moved from an indirect opening to a direct opening.

Change

The void of goodness is magnificent. It is a place where inner beauty takes hold without our being aware of it happening.

Every positive and miraculous self-discovery in our lives is brought about by change. Yet we continue to resist that which is inherent to our human nature. But when we seek out forms of entertainment (either a good book, a film, sports), we are excited and we anticipate the moment when something will change. We expect a quick delivery, the answer after the change, the point at which the sequence of events shifts, a moment where something happens. We want it to be there, we crave it. However, when faced with the opportunity for change in our own lives, very often we fear it, we deny it and will even try our best to avoid it.

So why do we settle? Why are we so afraid of change and openness? Are we conditioned, or in the habit of believing it is to be feared? "Better hold on to what I have. The change might be worse."

The reality is that change, when not forced or manipulated, is an aspect of freedom. Freedom is a void. Freedom is a burst of energy so pure that it is just *release*.

The Given, The Open-Ended

Outside of this Earth, *cycles* cannot exist because *time* does not exist. Truth, love and grace are not held in cycles, or in time. They do not have the laws of physics attached to them. They are pure; they just *are*. So when these attributes exist on this plane, on this Earth, they fall within our physical laws – in time. Truth, love and grace are infinite voids. They are able to work in any way, or in any direction the cycle wishes them to work because they exist *beyond* our world.

"Past here, the void is not a void.
The void is really an active space from here to there.
It takes us to a higher space, or a higher level.
The void pushes and it pulls; it gives and it takes us
to a finish line. That is the learning.
It has nothing to do with how things truly are.
Light and purity surpass a 'theory system' – like God.
We work with a system of pluses and minuses on this Earth
because it is a learning technique."

Death

Death : A permanent cessation of all vital functions : the end of life. The cause or occasion of loss of life.

The definition(s) in italics above are used by permission from Merriam-Webster Online Dictionary ©2004 by Merriam-Webster, Incorporated (www.Merriam-Webster.com).

The void of death is probably the most misunderstood passage for us as human beings. There is no way of working around this one.

What if we didn't have to?

Most religions and spiritual systems support the belief of an afterlife beyond this world, a type of reckoning or reward system – a heaven and a hell.

How do we really know that life exists past our earthly presence? There are reports from people who have had near-death experiences. Some say they have seen a light or have felt or seen the presence of angels, or of loved ones who have passed on before them. Some describe being enveloped in feelings of bliss or peace. Others give accounts of seeing an inter-dimensional space, or a system that appears as a grid.

But, do we really *know*? What if there is nothing? What if we just die?

The human species has been giving birth and dying on this Earth for at least several hundred thousand years. So why do we still have trouble accepting the fact that death is a purposeful opening? For a majority of people, death and illness are the two most unsettling and disturbing life processes. It should not be like that.

There is a concrete solution.

Through healing and cleansing, we will come to the realization that it is safe to be alone. When we allow a gap (an empty space between our human relationships and ourselves) to occur, we experience the humble void of solitude, which is a *death* from all other connections – a oneness with ourselves. We are then creating a void of "beyond Earth" while we are present here *on* Earth.

How many times have we experienced an original idea or a thought that just popped into our head out of the blue, one that did not have any apparent connection to what we were just thinking about? Or, felt a bond with another person we just met? This is energy, changing from one thought to another – or from one person to another. Every time we *invite* a new thought, idea or person into our lives, we allow for the existence of a gap between the old and new. We begin a process that will ultimately shed old thoughts, ideas or relationships. We are experiencing a death. We are making room for change. New energy appears, and there is a space made for it.

When we go to sleep, we experience a realm of non-consciousness, another level – a *death*, so to speak.

Have you ever been in an accident, or lost your sense of where you were through a traumatic moment? Perhaps there was a time when you were very ill; your energy shifted, it surrounded your body, it was not in your body anymore. You were *not here*. If the experience reached a very deep level, it was probably connected to a feeling of euphoria. Life took you for a ride away from yourself – away from your body. The vast wonder of the unknown has, in some way, revealed itself to you. If we remembered this, we would not be hindered by fear, and life itself would have more purpose. The experiences that we live through are all life and death. It is exciting, inventive, rewarding and freeing.

When we or those we love die, and they are there or on the *other side*, that is not the end. That is not just *it*. The positive emotional and spiritual connections with our loved ones do not come to an end. Love is present when there is a simultaneous or mutual feeling with another being. Love is pure, therefore, it is a true connection past this Earth. Our loved ones are not losing us, and we are not losing them. We will see and be with our loved ones again. There are many existences of reality.

Maybe death is the key to living life.

Science and spirituality are always mutually at work. Much of spiritual reasoning and thought can be broken down to a scientific base, or is compatible and consistent with our limited knowledge of science. But when God is added to the picture, scientific reasoning is no longer necessary. The reality of spirituality on this Earth is scientific, but when we go to the essence of spirituality, or to its outer circles, there is magic, because that is where God is.

Don't be afraid of death.
Death becomes the natural form of what life is about.
Through death we are exposed to God.
Death is the altered state that becomes present and concrete.
Then life, as we have known it, becomes the altered state.
Death is about reaching a much more expansive level.

God

God : 1 capitalized : the supreme or ultimate reality: as a : the Being perfect in power, wisdom, and goodness who is worshiped as creator and ruler of the universe b Christian Science : the incorporeal divine Principle ruling over all as eternal Spirit : infinite Mind. 2 : a being or object believed to have more than natural attributes and powers and to require human worship; specifically : one controlling a particular aspect or part of reality. 3 : a person or thing of supreme value. 4 : a powerful ruler

"Who's running the show?
Don't underestimate the power of God
or the force of that power."

"Trust that there is a plan. God has a plan for everything.
Why does life have surprises? It shifts to another level.
Life now."

God and The Humanness of God

When, as human beings, we try to imagine what God is, our perception and perspective molds God into a limited form of what each of us is capable of comprehending. We try to fit God into an advanced *superhuman* structure.

When there is dissension within us, our perception of anything that is pure, including God, is likely to be out of focus. Our image of God may differ from day to day. We are happy and faithful when God is "doing something for us," or is answering our prayers. But, when we experience a problem, or when things go wrong we ask, "If there is a God, why can't God see this, why is God so passive and not active?" We become angry or indignant when we think that God is asleep or is putting obstacles in front of us. Before we are fully healed, the barriers of denial and dilemma mire our vision.

We are in charge of our own lives. We orchestrate the highs, the lows and the teachings. Our life's journey is put in place by a higher part of ourselves. God is not human. Once we are whole, a clearer picture of God will be presented to us through ourselves and through this wholeness.

We are all united with God. We are all individual manifestations of God.

Let us imagine what God can be, and that probably is part of what God is. Imagine peace and security in a form of glory. Freedom and change are a part of love. Compassion, forgiveness and trust follow. Love on this Earth, to its deepest extent, is the closest feeling to establishing what God might be.

The fullness of God reaches far beyond our human comprehension. So most of the time, the concept of God needs to be introduced to us *through* the outside in, and this triggers-off our own inner connection with God. But, no matter what is given to us or what we have attained by our own searching, within and beyond our soul connection lies incomprehensible movement and answers.

God is wonder and tremendous passion.
God is the fire behind that passion.
God is the essence of water behind the ocean.
God is the wind without destruction and resistance.
God is the earth of all mankind.
God is the backbone of our true being,
but also the comfort and security we always need.

God wants to give us everything. God is active and solid. God's focus can be direct and minute. God is an intricate web of vulnerability. God can surpass detail and go to the direct source. God can manipulate space and time with such volume, strength and knowing that nothing escapes God. God sees it all. God is available to us to at all times. God is a puzzle within all that is justice. God is supreme understanding and intelligence.

Chapter 12

God is presence.
God is infinite home.
God is freedom.

CHAPTER 13

Outcome

"Discovery is the invention of life."

Outcome

*Outcome : Something that follows as a result or conse-
quence.*

The definition(s) in italics above are used by permission from Merriam-Webster Online Dictionary
©2004 by Merriam-Webster, Incorporated (www.Merriam-Webster.com).

*"This Earth is part of a child's playground, and we are
meant to be as children once more, but with responsibility.
So a part of our life should be about play and creation, and
part should be about a more graduated form of living.
Both should be exciting, enterprising and carefree."*

"A fresh start to a new life."

At the end of a healing journey there is creation,
beauty, uncompromised power, peace, adventure and worth.
This is a given.

The *outcome* is more.

When we feel unobstructed and clear and the surrounding situations of our life are reflecting this, we have
become whole.

Once we face the fact (even if it is just to ourselves)
that we do not feel well (physically, mentally, emotionally
or spiritually) we have moved into a field of knowledge and
healing. Life operates as a healer. Everyday in our lives,
circumstances and instances will be provided to bring us into

accomplishment and achievement. We set in perpetual motion that which will lead us from a beginning to an end.

The world will open itself to a place of natural healing once the individual heals.

When equilibrium between the self and the outer aspects (Earth) is created, then the new timing that we will live by, and our own clock *with* the Earth, will be in sync. This will create openings that we are not even aware of yet.

"It is the mending of time that brings clarity."

What holds us back?
- mission
- karma
- issues

"A mission is an order to be brought to order."

A mission is a task we are performing for the Earth itself, or it is a feat of accomplishment for the higher service of mankind. Whether a mission is conscious or subconscious, it always involves something more than just ourselves. It is a profound part of a healing journey and develops as life evolves. It is important in every life to carry out one's mission. We may be held back or detained while the mission unfolds. A mission is an unselfish act that has nothing to do with our own enjoyment of life. A mission may become part of our life to correct an injustice in ourselves, or it may be purity in action, as a sacrifice.

We are kept from becoming whole because of our karma, the to-do list that we made up before we came here. Karma may include a lesson.

The third thing keeping us from the outcome are the issues that we have not yet approached and/or totally worked through. This may be due to ignorance, denial, or an issue that is in the process of clearing.

Ultimate Healing is Brilliance

"Intelligence is only this; that we use and allow our uniqueness to work at its maximum and realize that every individual, including ourselves, has fault."

"Accomplishment is the essence of the human delivery. We feel good about stepping forward."

There is a time coming when this Earth will become valuable to us and we will become valuable to the Earth.

Each human being has the ability to unleash his or her own unique power. When possibilities are seen through healed eyes, they become reality.

"Promise is the purpose of passion."

Sameness and Differences

Once we have become humble, we accept that our sameness is a given; it is our foundation and our humanity. We have no fears about conforming, about being like everyone else in certain fundamental ways, about being human. And because we are not afraid, we grow into our uniqueness in an authentic natural manner. We have acquired the capacity to see a subject, and the world, in a totally different way from anyone else – *our* way. No one sees exactly what we see.

When we develop our diversity with this clear insight, our differences become our brilliance. The unique genius within each of us surfaces. When individuality assumes its correct role (raw in some ways, working out issues, not afraid to be shattered and altered) the soul will surface with a unique human being, which is our unique being. And from that release, the courage to be different without fear and with freedom will emerge.

When our individual differences are developed in a pure, non-egotistical way; they are exciting, non-competitive, adventurous and imaginative. When these pieces of ourselves are shared with a fellow human being, and their unique piece comes back to us, we not only learn about each other; we learn what matters. We are aware of new concepts, ideas and connections to another world that we have not yet explored in our own existence.

This is all part of an outcome.

The outcome equals self-delivery. The self-delivery occurs when life is brought back to us the way it should be.

We are brought to this planet to create a stage to achieve and to grow beyond what we have previously accomplished.

"The Outcome is to discover and applaud life
while we are living through life."

PART III

THE GAME
&
THE ART

CHAPTER 14

Circle of Change

The Game

Things change and change again.
Life as we know it is an illusion.
We fail, we climb, we fail.
We climb higher.
We win.
Don't fall off.
Hang on.

CIRCLE OF CHANGE

The Game of Life
Before and With the Joy of Life

How to Heal Anything

START/FINISH *"Good Stuff"*

Into the first stretch

Coming around the mountain, can I see home?

Circling towards the middle

I think I'm over the halfway point

Follow the formula on the next page to know how and where you are now and how your progress is unfolding. Begin at the point where you feel you should be. If you start at the wrong point, you will be shown quickly and you will be able to move.

THE GAME

The Healing Game goes around in a circle.
At each point you reach, you will notice either one,
or a combination of:
How you will feel.
What you should do.
What you are not going to like.

Starting Point

Just want it, think it or state it, "I want to be healed."
See, that was hard – but not so hard.
Whatever fits your lifestyle is the way that this phrase
should be understood.
"I want to be who I truly am."
"I want to be whole."
"I want to succeed without really trying."
"Hmm, hmm, hmm," but mean it.

Nothing will be taken away that is necessary for your
true happiness.

Into the First Stretch

The Universe at play – or – outer factors at play
"I'm afraid."
The voice of the Universe: "I hear you."

What you will be feeling and doing:
Giving up things you didn't think you could give up.
Being left out of sync and/or knowledge.
You may become upset over various uncontrollable
situations.
But, understand that the die is cast.
"I am moving forward."

Circling Towards the Middle

"I'm getting bored."
"I'm getting sick."
"I'm seeing things more clearly."
"I don't like it."
"I like it."
"I feel better deep inside, somehow."
"I'm still afraid…maybe…yes…uh…no…well, maybe."

I Think I'm Over the Halfway Point

At this juncture, you may be sent back for more learning.
Hold on. Hang in there. You are over the halfway point.

It is a trick of illusion.
"I feel like I'm at the beginning."
"When will this end?"

Coming Around the Mountain,
Can I See Home?

"I've given it all up."
"I feel some hope."
"Things are coming back in strange, noticeable, positive ways."
"I'm losing my fear."
"I feel stronger in my soul – deep down from somewhere inside myself."

The Finish

"If I need to learn, I will, but at the same time I am going forward."
"I am discovering, I am creating, and I am feeling."
"This is a world of teaching and a world of opportunity to reach and succeed far beyond where I have been."

The Strong Little Circle of Hope

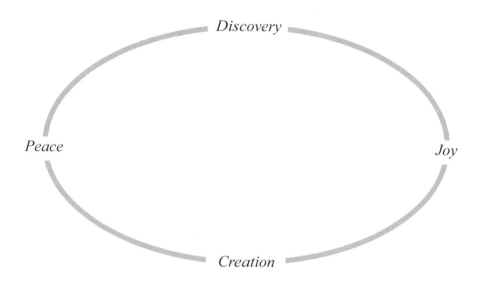

The Art

"This artwork has the ability to send peace through barriers."

Biographies

About the Authors

Christine A. Butler

Penney Leyshon

Penney Leyshon has maintained a private practice as a professional healer in New York City for twenty-five years. Penney has worked with thousands of clients from all walks of life and from all over the world. Many of her clients have no previous experience with a healer. Penney has sold hundreds of her original healing art pieces and products that she infuses with transformational properties. In addition to her personal healing practice, Penney Leyshon is a trusted business consultant.

Born in Staten Island, New York City, Penney is the eldest of five children. At the age of four and a half she was sexually abused in a school. This was the first event to open, fracture and prepare her soul to receive a most astonishing healing gift later in her life.

Penney's work experiences have been quite diverse. She worked in human resources and in finance on Wall Street. She spent ten years assisting in the supervision of a recovery room at a women's health crisis facility, where she was counselor to hundreds of patients each week.

Shy, yet of independent spirit, Penney was never "one of the pack" in any arena of her life. As far back as she can remember, Penney had an inner wisdom that was vastly unique. She was in touch with, and felt the power of, a higher intelligence. Penney knew extraordinary things, but did not know why or what it was all leading up to. She did know, however, that somehow the body and mind heal themselves.

When she was twenty-nine years old, Penney began an eight-year struggle with anorexia. At the age of thirty-three, and intensely undernourished at a weight of seventy pounds, she went through a breakdown. It was at this time that her immense healing gift was revealed. While walking through a woodland area in northern New Jersey, a light came from the ground and went in through her eyes. She walked away knowing she was a healer. When her life took this turn, she felt her inner knowledge begin to make sense. Penney knew exactly what to do. It was as if this day had always been expected.

Penney studied Shiatsu massage privately for six years and attended the Ohashi Institute in New York City for one year. She then attended and received her massage license from The Swedish Institute, a New York State board-certified massage school.

An amazing experience took place in Penney's life at the age of forty-two. Penney Leyshon endured an incomprehensible event that changed her way of life completely.

"...I saw the Earth from the beginning of itself and past there. I saw the universe and past there. All of the past came flooding in and through. I witnessed it through me... second by second of terror and pain, mine and that of humanity. I became so alert that the vibration of sound altered me, and presented different realities that sent me into and through horrific episodes. It was massive panic, and yet holy. It captured me. This period was devastating. Yet, somehow I kept on functioning around it, in life. I got up, I ate, walked, bathed, but I didn't understand why or what was going on. I just knew that it was happening for some deep reason...some type of purpose. I knew that I must stay with it. It was certainly staying with me. Time, for me, has been altered and the work has advanced."

Penney's being yawns open to the universe and vibrates with it. She sees what is out there. She works with it and filters it through her.

Penney Leyshon has finished the first book in her children's series, "Perisma," and is currently working on three other literary projects. She and Kathleen Spellman de'Rossi have formed Oxccidus, a company dedicated to publishing, inventing and games.

Christine A. Butler

Kathleen Spellman

Kathleen brings a broad view of the world, its peoples and their universal concerns to the writing of this book. She was born in Oak Park, Illinois, the eldest of seven. At the age of fourteen, her family moved from Harrison, New York to Vienna, Austria where she spent her high school years learning languages, traveling and meeting fellow students from fifty countries around the world. She graduated Magna Cum Laude from Manhattan College with a degree in international studies and economics. Kathleen is proficient in German, French, Spanish and Italian. Her exposure to, and passion for, an international world continues to shape her life.

Her diverse work experience has sent her on a journey of discovery around the globe. She spent time as a teacher in Guatemala, as a reinsurance portfolio manager at a major international insurance company, a marketer of independent films for a Brazilian production company, and as a personal organizer. Kathleen is currently working on two additional non-fiction projects and developing a series of games with Penney Leyshon for their company, Oxccidus. She is also writing a novel. Kathleen is the mother of three children and lives with her family in Norwalk, Connecticut.

"Kathleen Spellman is a woman of substance, strength, wisdom and capability. She is my partner in writing this book. A seer of honest vision is what I would look for in a collaborator. Kathy has all of this and more. Her skill as an interpreter far surpasses four world languages. She combines her earthly knowledge with her spiritual insights, and her ability has afforded an opportunity for me to express the truths that I feel come through me. Because Kathy is always seeking the truth, and looking for the next door to open, our collaboration was of little effort. With her uncompromising energy juggling her family, establishing our business and writing this book, she has left little uncovered."

Penney Leyshon

INDEX

A Gift of Healing

IN A HANDBOOK

If you would like to order additional copies of
"A Gift of Healing in a Handbook" or to find out
information about other Oxccidus products,
please visit our website at:
http://www.oxccidus.com

or contact us at:

Oxccidus LLC
P.O. Box 274
Rowayton, CT
06853

info@oxccidus.com